SAVED FROM WHAT?

SAVED
FROM
WHAT?

R. C. Sproul

CROSSWAY BOOKS

A DIVISION OF
GOOD NEWS PUBLISHERS
WHEATON, ILLINOIS

Saved from What?

Copyright © 2002 by R. C. Sproul

Published by Crossway Books
   a division of Good News Publishers
   1300 Crescent Street
   Wheaton, Illinois 60187

Cover design: UDG / DesignWorks, Sisters, Oregon

First printing 2002

Printed in the United States of America

Unless otherwise marked, Scripture references are from the New King James Version. Copyright © 1982, Thomas Nelson, Inc. Used by permission.

Scripture references marked NIV are from the Holy Bible: New International Version.® Copyright © 1973, 1978, 1984 by International Bible Society. Used by permission of Zondervan Publishing House. All rights reserved.

The "NIV" and "New International Version" trademarks are registered in the United States Patent and Trademark Office by International Bible Society. Use of either trademark requires the permission of International Bible Society.

Library of Congress Cataloging-in-Publication Data
Sproul, R. C. (Robert Charles), 1939–
 Saved from What? / R. C. Sproul.
  p. cm.
 Includes bibliographical references and index.
 ISBN 1-58134-417-1 (hc : alk. paper)
 1. Redemption. I. Title.
BT775 .S68 2002
234—dc21   2002004434
                  CIP

15	14	13	12	11	10	09	08	07	06	05	04	03	02
15	14	13	12	11	10	9	8	7	6	5	4	3	2	1

For Dave and Maureen Buchman
Friends, colaborers, and kinsmen in the faith

Contents

Publisher's Foreword

THIS MAY BE THE MOST important book that you will ever read in your life. Why? Because the question that it asks (and answers)—"Saved from What?"—is the most important question anyone will ever face.

There are four possible ways that this question could relate to you. First, you may not be saved and you realize that you are not—and if this is the case you are in grave danger.

Second, you may not be saved and you think that you are. In this case you would be in even greater danger because you are unaware of the great danger you are in—and I urge you to read this book and to understand the desperate situation that you are in.

Third, you may be saved but you are unclear about what this means. In this case, I would also urge you to read this book because in these pages you will find great assurance and joy.

Lastly, you may be saved and already have assurance and understanding concerning your salvation. In this case, reading this book can become an occasion for a deeper relationship with God and for a new sense of joy and gratitude to God.

What then is this book about? First it is about the desperate, utterly hopeless, eternally lost condition of every person who is not saved and who therefore lives under the righteous condemnation and wrath of God.

But more than this, it is a book that spells out clearly and powerfully the "great salvation" that God has provided in the life, death, and resurrection of His only Son, Jesus Christ—how through faith in Christ, and in His work on our behalf, we have forgiveness of our sin and freedom from guilt; and how we now stand righteous before God, the holy judge and creator of all that exists.

But even more than this, it is a book that gives an unforgettable glimpse into eternity, into heaven, and into the indescribable joy and beauty and glory that awaits all who are saved.

I invite you then to read these pages. And I pray that as a result you will understand—either for the first time or in a new and transforming way—the "great salvation" that God has provided through faith in Christ, the only Son of God, who died for our sins.

To this end, then, may this be the most important book you will ever read.

—Lane T. Dennis, Ph.D.
President and Publisher
Crossway Books

PART I

Saved *from* What?

1

Saved *from* What?

"ARE YOU SAVED?"

I recall vividly a time more than three decades ago, in 1969, when I was asked this question.

These were the volatile days of the sixties—the era of the cultural revolution in America. I was a professor of theology at the Conwell School of Theology on the campus of Temple University in Philadelphia. The days were anything but halcyon. They were turbulent, marked by demonstrations against the war in Vietnam. Paroxysms of rage punctuated student protests and sit-ins. The academic world was in a state of unprecedented turmoil and upheaval. I recall trying to lecture above the din of bullhorns outside the classroom windows as I competed with the S.D.S. (Students for a Democratic Society) for my students' attention.

On one such day I sought an hour's solace and quietude from this cacophony in the faculty dining room. I stretched my lunch hour to the limit in order to squeeze out every moment of peace I could enjoy.

As the noon hour ended, I deposited my lunch tray in the bin and began my trek across the plaza to my classroom. I was walking briskly to avoid being late. I was alone, minding my own business. Suddenly, apparently out of nowhere, a gentleman appeared in front of me, blocking my forward progress. He looked me in the eye and asked directly, "Are you saved?"

I wasn't quite sure how to respond to this intrusion. I uttered in response the first words that came into my mind: "Saved from what?" What I was thinking, but had the grace not to say, was, "I'm certainly not saved from strangers buttonholing me and asking me questions like yours." But when I said, "Saved from what?" I think the man who stopped me that day was as surprised by my question as I had been by his. He began to stammer and stutter. Obviously he wasn't quite sure how to respond.

"Saved from what? Well, you know what I mean. You know, do you know Jesus?" Then he tried to give me a brief summary of the gospel.

This serendipitous encounter left an impression on me. I experienced real ambivalence. On the one hand, I was delighted in my soul that someone cared enough about me, even though I was a stranger, to stop me and ask about my salvation. But it was clear that, though this man had a zeal for salvation, he had little understanding of what salvation is. He was using Christian jargon. The words fell from his lips without being processed by his mind. As a result, his words were empty of content. Clearly, the man had a love for Christ and a concern for people. Few Christians have the courage to engage perfect strangers in evangelistic discussion. But sadly, he had little understanding of what he was so zealously trying to communicate.

DO EVANGELICALS UNDERSTAND THE GOSPEL?

But what about the church today? Do evangelical Christians today have any clearer understanding of the gospel, of what it means to be saved? Sadly, again, there often seems to be little understanding even among those who are most active in evangelical circles.

Take for example a survey conducted by Christians United for Reformation (CURE) among the delegates to the annual convention of the Christian Booksellers Association some years ago. Since the delegates are comprised mostly of Christians, we would think that they would have a basic grasp of the essential truths of the gospel. But when CURE staff asked one hundred delegates at random, the staff found that only one of those who were polled gave an "adequate" definition of the gospel. Most of the answers were something like, "The gospel is having a personal relationship with Jesus," or, "It means asking Jesus into your heart." Absent from these definitions were any affirmations of the person and work of Christ and the appropriation of His work to the individual by faith alone.

The sampling in the poll was small—only one hundred from over five thousand. Perhaps the answers were skewed by how the question was asked. But after talking with the pollsters, I was left shocked by the apparent ignorance of the most elementary article of Christianity.

As it turned out, I was asked to preach at the Sunday morning worship service for the next Christian Booksellers Convention, a year later. With the results of the CURE survey still in mind, I decided to speak on the theme of salvation, asking the question, "What is salvation?" I was nervous about the selection of this topic. I had two fears. I feared that asking such a basic question of Christian publishers and booksellers would seem like carrying coals to Newcastle, that it would seem to them a waste of time to consider something they already knew fully. And I feared that by addressing such a basic matter I would be insulting the intelligence of my hearers and would come across as patronizing or downright rude.

When I finished the sermon that morning, I was overwhelmed by the response. All week long people came up to thank me, saying things like, "I never thought of it like that." Indeed, I have attended every CBA convention since that year, and at every single one of them people have mentioned that sermon to me. If you are not a preacher, you might miss the significance of that. Rarely do people comment on sermons they heard from our lips in times past. I hardly remember myself what I preached on three weeks ago. My congregation would naturally remember even less. The power of the word is not in people's being able to summarize a message they've heard. Rather, it is the power of God's Word piercing the soul. With that in mind, let me reproduce here the full Bible text from my only sermon from the book of the prophet Zephaniah—the only time during almost forty years that I can remember preaching from Zephaniah, but a profoundly shocking text that uniquely answers the question, "Saved from what?" The text reads:

> The great day of the LORD is near;
> It is near and hastens quickly.
> The noise of the day of the LORD is bitter;
> There the mighty men shall cry out.
>   That day is a day of wrath,
> A day of trouble and distress,
> A day of devastation and desolation,
> A day of darkness and gloominess,
> A day of clouds and thick darkness,
>   A day of trumpet and alarm

Against the fortified cities
And against the high towers.

"I will bring distress upon men,
And they shall walk like blind men,
Because they have sinned against the LORD;
Their blood shall be poured out like dust,
And their flesh like refuse."

Neither their silver nor their gold
Shall be able to deliver them
In the day of the LORD's wrath;
But the whole land shall be devoured
By the fire of His jealousy,
For He will make speedy riddance
Of all those who dwell in the land (Zephaniah 1:14-18).

If we read this text carefully, we will easily see that it has precious little "gospel" in it. The message is not "good news" but horrific news. It is so dire that one is not surprised when it is relegated to a hidden corner of the pastor's study. The message is not politically correct in our time. The descriptive terms Zephaniah uses to paint the picture of the day of the Lord include the following:

bitter	devastation	darkness
trouble	refuse	devoured
alarm	desolation	gloominess
distress	wrath	fire
blood		

It seems almost as if the Holy Spirit enlarged Zephaniah's vocabulary to make the point clear. The litany of descriptive terms leaves little doubt about the horror of this predicted day. And this passage is but a small portion of the prophecy. The full message is even more hair-raising in its graphic declaration of the outpouring of God's wrath.

To be sure, the end of Zephaniah's book gives the divine promise of redemption. It ends on a high note, but not before stressing the dreadful exposure of the nation to the stark reality of divine judgment.

With a message so grim, what would even incline me to want to preach from this text? Simply this: here in this seldom preached passage we have the clearest descriptions in the Bible in answer to the question, "Saved from what?" And when we're talking about salvation, we are talking about the concept that is *the central theme of all of sacred Scripture*—a concept that it is imperative to understand.

THE MEANING OF SALVATION

When we search the Scriptures to determine the meaning of the term *salvation,* the first thing we notice is that it is used in a wide variety of ways. All sorts of things are discussed in connection with the noun *salvation* or the verb *to save.*

For example, I have often wondered why, when God delivered Paul and Silas from the jail in Philippi by the earthquake, the jailer in panic came up to them and asked, "Sirs, what must I do to be saved?" Paul responded immediately by saying, "Believe on the Lord Jesus Christ, and you will be saved, you and your household" (Acts 16:30-31). I think I know what Paul meant by salvation when he responded to the jailer, but I have wondered what was in the jailer's mind when he asked his question. Here was a man who was responsible to the government for the guarding of prisoners, and the law in that day was simply this: if prisoners escaped from the jail, whatever penalty they were to suffer for their crimes, their jailer had to take that penalty in their place. When the walls of the jail fell down and the prisoners started to run free, this jailer ran to Paul and Silas and asked them about salvation.

It is certainly possible that what he had in his mind at that moment was a question about his eternal destiny, about his relationship with God. He had heard Paul and Silas singing hymns, and he knew they were religious fellows. The jailer addressed his question to the greatest theologian in history, the apostle Paul: "What must I do to be saved?" Maybe he had eternity in view. Or perhaps all the Philippian jailer had in his mind was, how am I going to escape from the consequences of this jailbreak? The word *salvation* in the Bible doesn't always refer to the ultimate question of being reconciled with God.

A woman came to Jesus for healing and beseeched Him to cure her of her disease. With a touch Jesus healed her and said, "Go in peace. Your faith has saved you." They didn't even talk about reconciliation with God. The woman was looking for relief from pain and sickness. She was trying to be saved from the ravages of disease, and Jesus saved her from that. When Jesus said, "Your faith has saved you," He may have meant it in the ultimate sense, but it's also possible that He did not. Once again, when the Bible uses the word *salvation* or the verb *to save,* it doesn't necessarily refer to what we mean by the *doctrine* of salvation.

The Bible says that women will be "saved" through childbirth (1 Timothy 2:15). Paul also teaches the Corinthians that "the unbelieving husband is sanctified by the wife, and the unbelieving wife is sanctified by the husband" (1 Corinthians 7:14). Does this mean that the New Testament teaches three ways of salvation: 1) having personal faith in Christ; 2) marrying somebody who has faith in Christ; and 3) for women, childbearing? You don't even have to marry somebody who is a Christian; just have a baby and you're in the kingdom of God?

Obviously, we know that that is not what the Bible teaches. The Bible uses the term *salvation* in many ways. Not every time the word is used does it refer to our reconciliation with God. The common thread that is found in the many uses is that, at its root, "salvation" means being rescued or delivered from some calamity or catastrophe.

When the Jewish people went into battle against the Philistines, it looked as if they were going to lose until finally the tide of the battle changed and they emerged victorious. In this case the Jew would speak of being "saved." A person who recovered from a life-threatening disease likewise spoke of being "saved," having been rescued from a calamity. Even in our own culture we speak this way. If a boxer is knocked to the canvas and the referee is interrupted by the bell at the count of nine, we say that the boxer has been "saved by the bell." We don't mean that the boxer has now been ushered by the angels into the kingdom of heaven. We mean that he has been spared from the calamity of defeat, at least temporarily, until the next round begins.

The broad meaning of salvation in Scripture is to be saved from calamity, such as war, disease, death, or other perils. But there is one calamity, one catastrophe so utterly grim that rescue from it is the essence of the biblical doctrine of salvation. That catastrophe will be described shortly. But first, one other thing needs to be noted by way of introduction.

SALVATION: PAST, PRESENT, FUTURE

We have seen that the word *salvation* is used in several senses. And the verb *to save* is used in several tenses. That's easy to remember: several senses, several tenses. The Greek language has more verb tenses than we have in English. "To save" is found in the New Testament in every possible sense and in every possible tense of the Greek verb. The Bible speaks of our having been saved from the foundation of the world (Ephesians 1:4). Here the ultimate past tense is used in regard to salvation. So in one narrow sense, at least, from all eternity in the hidden wisdom of God, we were saved. That is why Jesus says that there will come a moment when the King will say, "Come, you blessed of My Father, inherit the kingdom prepared for you from the foundation of the world" (Matthew 25:34).

But the Bible also uses the imperfect tense and says there is a sense in which we *were being saved,* that salvation from the hands of God for His people is something that He has been working at through all of the pages of history. We were a part of the Exodus in the plan of God's redemption. Our salvation was being prepared for us through the call of Abraham, and in the lives of Isaac and of Jacob we were being saved.

The Bible also speaks of salvation in the present tense. There is a sense in which we *are* saved. The moment we put our trust in Christ and in Christ alone—at that moment God pronounces us justified in His sight. He transfers the righteousness of Christ to our account. We are safe in the arms of Jesus. We are now in a state of salvation.

The Bible also says that we *are being saved.* Salvation is not simply a once-for-all thing. Salvation begins when I have belief; as I grow in grace and in sanctification, that process of sanctification is also described as a process of salvation.

Finally, the Bible speaks of the future when we *shall be saved.* We are saved. We are being saved. We shall be saved as we look forward to our glorification together with Christ and the final consummation of our salvation. So we can see from this how easy it is to become confused about what the Bible means by salvation. Different senses. Different tenses.

SAVED FROM THE WRATH TO COME

When we explore the ultimate sense of salvation, we must return to the question I asked the man in Philadelphia so many years ago: "Saved from what?" In his First Epistle to the Thessalonians Paul writes:

> For they themselves declare concerning us what manner of entry we had to you, and how you turned to God from idols to serve the living and true God, and to wait for His Son from heaven, whom He raised from the dead, even Jesus who delivers us from the wrath to come (1 Thessalonians 1:9-10).

What is this "wrath" that is to come? Some scholars believe it is a cryptic reference to the impending doom of Jerusalem that occurred in A.D. 70. Others see it as a reference to the last judgment.

The ultimate salvation that any human being can ever experience is rescue from the wrath that is to come. Do we believe that there remains a wrath that is to come? I think the greatest point of unbelief in our culture and in our church today is an unbelief in the wrath of God and in His certain promise of judgment for the human race.

I talk to people about Jesus frequently. They say to me things like, "R. C., if you find believing in Jesus meaningful, if that turns you on, if it gives you some kind of solace or whatever, then that's fine for you. But I don't feel the need for Jesus."

What are they saying? It's like somebody who says he doesn't feel the need for a fireman because his house is not on fire. Who needs a fireman when there's no fire? Who needs a Savior when there's no clear and present threat of judgment? People today simply do not believe that there will be a day of judgment. But if we believed it, really believed it, the energy of our evangelism would increase a hundredfold.

In the Old Testament the fundamental difference between the true prophet and the false prophet was that the true prophet proclaimed the day of the Lord as a day of consuming wrath. The people didn't want to hear that, so the false prophet received applause by promising the people that the day of the Lord was a day of brightness and light and joy, that there was nothing to worry about. "God loves you." "God has a wonderful plan for your life." But the reality is that God does not have a wonderful plan for the impenitent. To such people, God's plan won't look good at all on the day of judgment. God will speak then in His fury. That was the message of Isaiah, of Jeremiah, of Ezekiel, of Daniel, of Micah, of Amos, indeed of every prophet of God. Amos came to the people and declared:

> Woe to you who desire the day of the LORD!
> For what good is the day of the LORD to you?
> It will be darkness, and not light.
> It will be as though a man fled from a lion,

And a bear met him!
Or as though he went into the house,
Leaned his hand on the wall,
And a serpent bit him!
Is not the day of the LORD darkness, and not light?
Is it not very dark, with no brightness in it? (Amos 5:18-20).

Christians get excited about the return of Jesus. Oh, happy day! Yes, it is a happy day for the saved, but for the unsaved the return of Jesus is the worst of all conceivable calamities. It is a day of desolation, as the prophet Zephaniah foretold. Near is the great day of the Lord. Near, coming very quickly. A day of wrath is that day, a day of trouble, of distress, destruction, desolation, darkness, gloom. And on the day of the Lord's wrath all of the earth will be devoured, for He will make a terrifying end to the inhabitants of this world (see Zephaniah 1:14-18).

Saved from what? As Paul wrote to the Thessalonians, he understood that a savior is one who rescues us from a great, indeed, the greatest, calamity (see 1 Thessalonians 1:10). Jesus is the Savior who saves us from the wrath that is to come.

SALVATION *OF* AND *FROM* THE LORD

At the core of the biblical message of salvation is another concept often obscured in modern thought. Salvation is *of* the Lord. No human being has the resources, the power, the money, or the merit to save himself. The necessary power for rescue is not in us. It must come from God. Salvation is of the Lord because only the Lord can accomplish it.

A few years ago I was in the hospital for kidney stones. If you have ever had kidney stones, you know what catastrophe means. It was Christmastime, and I was lying in my bed and looking up at the television set on the wall. Spinning the dial, I came to a worship service that was coming from a church in California. The pastor was reading the Christmas story from Luke. I had heard this text read a multitude of times. "For there is born to you this day in the city of David a Savior, who is Christ the Lord" (Luke 2:11). As I heard the story this time I said to myself, "Oh, that is what I need right now. I need a savior." My soul was fine, but my kidney needed to be saved and fast. At that moment God had my undivided attention, and I knew I was in need of rescue.

The doctors rescued me from my calamity, but the only person who can rescue anybody from the wrath that is to come is God's appointed Savior; the only salvation that ultimately matters is *of* the Lord. However, when the Scriptures tell us that God saves us, that salvation is *of* the Lord, we tend to forget that salvation is also *from* the Lord.

What do we need to be saved from? We need to be saved *from God*—not from kidney stones, not from hurricanes, not from military defeats. What every human being needs to be saved *from* is God. The last thing in the world the impenitent sinner ever wants to meet on the other side of the grave is God. But the glory of the gospel is that the One from whom we need to be saved is the very One who saves us. God in saving us saves us from Himself.

Woe unto those who have no Savior on the day of wrath. The Bible says that on that day the unbeliever will scream to the mountains to fall upon him, to the hills to hide him. People will be looking for refuge from nature itself, crying, "Cover me! Give me a shield!" But there is only one Shield that can protect anyone from the wrath that is to come. It is the covering of the righteousness of Christ.

When we put our faith in Jesus, God cloaks us with the garments of Jesus, and the garments of Christ's righteousness are never, ever the target of God's wrath. He who flees to Jesus has peace with God, and there is no condemnation left.

When calamity struck in the days of Noah, the day of the Lord came and almost all of the world perished in the flood. But for Noah and his family the day of the Lord was their day of salvation. For the unbeliever, the day of the Lord is a day of darkness with no light in it. For the Christian, the day of the Lord is a day of light with no darkness in it.

Are you saved? That question is the most important issue any person will ever face.

When we consider even for a moment the frightening dimension of the unbridled outpouring of God's wrath, we tremble in our souls. When we consider that we deserve to be consumed by His fury and realize that His fury has instead consumed Jesus in our place, when we recognize the greatness of the peril, we then are able to see the greatness of the salvation that He has bestowed upon us. How shall we escape if we neglect so great a salvation?

2

The Shattered Self-image

THAT WE ARE SHOCKED by the idea that we are saved *from* God reveals two crucial shortcomings in our understanding. We fail to understand who God is, and we fail to understand who we are. Our view of God is too low, and our view of mankind is too high. This was Isaiah's painful discovery when he got a glimpse of the unveiled holiness of God. In that encounter Isaiah understood for the first time in his life who God is. It was also the first time he understood who he was. He cursed himself, crying, "Woe is me, for I am undone! Because I am a man of unclean lips" (Isaiah 6:5).

Isaiah's discovery shattered his self-image. His vision of God made him come apart at the seams. And his experience was not unique in the biblical record. It seems that every person who encounters the living God in Scripture suddenly loses his self-composure and experiences a severe identity crisis. The ego is shattered into tiny pieces.

We live in one of the most narcissistic cultures of all time. In Greek mythology Narcissus saw a reflection of himself in the clear water of a pond and fell in love with his own image. What he did was mythical. What we do is real.

A few years ago an international study measured the correlation between proficiency in mathematics and the students' feelings about their performances. American students finished seventh—dead last—in mathematical proficiency. At the same time, however, the Americans finished first in their positive feelings about their performance. It seems our students are learning self-esteem better than they're grasping math! We are teaching people how to have a good self-image while performing badly.

SELF-ESTEEM AND THE HOLINESS OF GOD

The narcissistic quest has worked. We are not worried about the wrath of God because we have discounted the severity of our sin. Our self-esteem is a shield protecting our eyes from God's holiness. Meanwhile, throughout Scripture we find the pattern of God shattering human egos. We see it in the experience not only of Isaiah but of several others.

Consider the case of King Belshazzar. When he held his great feast in which he boasted of his victories over Israel and mocked God by drinking from the holy vessels, he was suddenly interrupted:

> In the same hour the fingers of a man's hand appeared and wrote opposite the lampstand on the plaster of the wall of the king's palace; and the king saw the part of the hand that wrote (Daniel 5:5).

Daniel goes on to describe the king's reaction:

> Then the king's countenance changed, and his thoughts troubled him, so that the joints of his hips were loosened

and his knees knocked against each other. The king cried aloud . . . (Daniel 5:6-7).

When the hand of God appeared, "the king's countenance changed." The changing of the countenance was directly connected to his troubling thoughts. Though he didn't know at that point what the words meant, he surely knew it was not good news; God was not writing the gospel on the wall. Belshazzar was so devastated that his joints came loose, and he became literally knock-kneed.

In an instant the king's confidence was ruined, his arrogance destroyed. His self-image burst asunder. And as the writing foretold, he didn't survive the day. His kingdom fell and he was slain that very night.

THE SEVERITY OF SIN

When I submitted a manuscript for one of my children's books to a Christian publisher, the editor changed all of my references to "sin." The term "sin" was changed to "making poor choices." I inquired of the editor why the changes were made. The editor replied, "We don't want to give children a poor self-image."

The best self-image we can ever have is one that is accurate and true. The Bible makes it clear that we have value as creatures made in the image of God. We affirm the sanctity of human life because every person is made in God's image. But that image has been tarnished. It has been desecrated by sin.

As long as we discount the severity of our sin, we sense no fear of God. We are content with our performance as it is, deluding ourselves into believing it is good enough to satisfy a holy God. This was precisely the condition of the rich young ruler who approached Jesus (Luke 18:18-23).

The young man was excited. He had heard Jesus talk about the kingdom of God, and his interest was kindled. He rushed to Jesus and inquired, "Good Teacher, what shall I do to inherit eternal life?" Obviously he was intrigued by the idea of living forever. He thought that sounded great. He wanted to sign up for it immediately. How did Jesus respond to him? What were the first words out of His mouth? Jesus looked at the man and said, "Why do you call Me good? No one is good but One, that is, God."

Critics have jumped on Jesus' answer and have used it to argue against the sinless perfection of Christ. They take His words to indicate a denial both of His goodness and of His deity. But that is not what Jesus was saying. Jesus understood that the young man had no idea to whom he was speaking. He came to Christ in a cavalier way, a frivolous way, armed with a superficial understanding of goodness. Perhaps in his flattering words he was trying to enhance Jesus' self-esteem. But Jesus would have none of it. He confronted the man in his tracks: "Why are you calling Me good? Don't you know only God is good?"

Jesus knew the young ruler did not recognize Him as God incarnate. Since he did not know he was talking to the God-man, his superficial use of the term *good* was apparent. We notice that Jesus did not challenge the ruler's simplistic understanding of *good* directly. Rather, in Socratic fashion Jesus endeavored to challenge him by a series of questions. He reminded the man of the Law. He took him straight to the Ten Commandments.

"You know the commandments: 'Do not commit adultery,' 'Do not murder,' 'Do not steal,' 'Do not bear false witness,' 'Honor your father and your mother.'" And [the young ruler] said, "All these things I have kept from my youth" (Luke 18:20-21).

The man's response to Jesus betrayed disappointment. Evidently he was expecting a profound spiritual secret from the lips of Christ. He wasn't interested in the traditional answers he had heard from the rabbis: "Thou shalt not kill. Thou shalt not steal. Thou shalt not commit adultery. Keep the Law." He said, "Jesus, I've been keeping these commandments all my life." At this point Jesus could have said, "I guess you weren't present when I preached the Sermon on the Mount and explained the full meaning of the Law. If you understood the Law as I have revealed it, you would realize you haven't kept a single one of the commandments since you got out of your bed this morning." But Jesus didn't do that. Instead of telling the man he had not kept the Law, He *showed* him. In a sense He took him straight to the first commandment about having no other gods. He instructed the fellow to sell his goods and give all to the poor. The man walked away sorrowfully, for he was very rich. He failed the test on the first commandment.

It is amazing how many "rich young rulers" there are in the world and the church today. Multitudes are secure that their destination is heaven because they think they have kept the Ten Commandments. They don't understand that by the works of the Law no flesh will ever be justified in the sight of God (see Galatians 2:16). If we think we can make it into heaven by keeping the Law, we are under the worst of all possible delusions. If we live by the Law, we will die by the Law.

GOD'S PERFECT STANDARD

I was speaking to a lady recently who related an experience with her son. The son was about six years old. The mother is very keen on evangelism, so she asked her son, "Do you think that after you grow up and live your life and die, you're going to go to heaven?" The boy seemed fairly confident that he would go to heaven, and so the mother probed just a little bit and asked, "Well, suppose you were to stand before God, and He looked you straight in the eye and said, 'Why should I let you into My heaven?'—what would you say to God?" The little boy thought for a second, and then looked up at his mother and said, "Well, if God asked me that, I would say, 'Because I really tried hard to be good.'" Then a puzzled look came over his face for a moment, and he said, "Well . . . , not that good."

I thought that was perceptive for a six-year-old child, because most of us harbor in our minds the feeling that all it's going to take to make us acceptable to God on the day of judgment is that we have tried, that we have done our best, and that we have been basically good. But even a six-year-old child with a limited understanding of God's perfection and an immature understanding of his own fallenness had to think twice. He realized that his goodness was not quite good enough.

In fact, "not quite good enough" is an understatement. We are not even *close* to being good enough. I would say the greatest and most frequent error that human beings make is the assumption that they are going to survive the judgment of a holy God on the basis of their own performance.

What would you say to God if He asked you, "Why should I let you into My heaven?" How would you answer that? How do you hope to stand before God? This calls attention to the problem of our fallenness. The six-year-old boy who said that he tried to be good but realized he wasn't good enough was working with another faulty assumption. He was thinking of his own sin as being merely on the surface, something that slightly marred the image of God; but he lacked an accurate understanding of the degree and intensity of his alienation from God. All of us admit that no one is perfect. If I ask people if they are sinners, virtually all of them admit that they are. They often say, "Nobody's perfect." To be a sinner doesn't seem a serious matter to them. After all, "to err is human, to forgive, divine." The adage almost drips with the assumption that since God is divine, He is obligated to forgive us.

No Fear of God

Part of the reason that we never achieve the standard of righteousness or perfection that God requires of us, that none of us mirrors or reflects His greatness, is that we don't understand what the standard is. We are so far removed in our thinking from God's holiness that we have become blinded to what sin is. We live in a culture where all of us do what is right in our own eyes, forgetting that it is the eye of God that determines what is good.

Paul describes our fallen nature in Romans 3:

> As it is written: "There is none righteous, no, not one;
>   There is none who understands;
> There is none who seeks after God.
>   They have all turned aside;
> They have together become unprofitable;
> There is none who does good, no, not one."
>   "Their throat is an open tomb;

With their tongues they have practiced deceit";
"The poison of asps is under their lips";
  "Whose mouth is full of cursing and bitterness."
  "Their feet are swift to shed blood;
  Destruction and misery are in their ways;
  And the way of peace they have not known."
  "There is no fear of God before their eyes" (Romans 3:10-18).

Paul reaches the bottom line: "There is no fear of God before their eyes." Do we fear God? Do we have a sense of honor and reverence for Him? Do Paul's words seem utterly strange and foreign to us? God made us, and He made us in His image. In making us in His image, He has built into our human makeup a capacity and a need to reverence our Creator. We know that God is worthy of our honor, our reverence, and our adoration. We know that it is our moral responsibility to give Him these things. But we have been disobedient for so long that we no longer even fear God. We laugh at Him. We think that He can't touch us or hurt us. That is how deep our sin goes. It is not just on the surface. It is not simply that we've missed the mark, that we are alienated from God, but that, in our natural state, we are actually enemies of God.

We arrive in this world fallen. Because of our fall in Adam, we are born with a corrupt nature. This is what is meant by "original sin." Original sin is not the sin that Adam and Eve committed. It is the *result* of that first sin. Original sin has reference to our sinful condition, our sinful bent, our sinful inclination from which actual sin flows. In other words, *we sin because we are sinners.* We are not sinners because we sin. Since the fall of mankind it is now the nature of human beings to be inclined and drawn to sinfulness. I sin because I am a sinner.

David said, "I was brought forth in iniquity, and in sin did my mother conceive me" (Psalm 51:5).

Saint Augustine is perhaps best known for his prayer, "O Lord, Thou hast made us for Thyself, and our hearts are restless until they find their rest in Thee." But one of his lesser-known prayers provoked one of the most serious controversies in the history of theology. Augustine prayed, "God, grant what Thou commandest, and command what Thou dost desire." For a theologian to say, "O God, command what You want," would certainly not make history; but the other part of the prayer—"Grant what You command of us"—did set off a firestorm. Why would Augustine ask God to give to us that which He commands from us? What Augustine was wrestling with was the severity of our fallen condition. On the one hand, God says, "Be perfect." He commands perfection, and yet we are born in a state of corruption that makes it morally impossible for us by our own strength or ability to do what God commands. We can be obedient to the commandments of God only if God helps us in the process by extending His grace to us and by enabling us to do what He calls us to do. That is what Augustine had in mind when he said, "Grant what You command of us."

When a certain monk became agitated by Augustine's statement, the matter escalated into a major theological controversy. The monk who reacted against Augustine's prayer was named Pelagius. Pelagius argued that God never commands the impossible. God's requirement of perfection from us must mean that we have the ability to perform with perfect righteousness. Whatever else the fall did to man, said Pelagius, it did not take away our ability to achieve perfection. If God commands perfection from fallen sinners, then we certainly must have the ability to achieve perfection. Pelagius argued that grace makes righteousness easier for us, but it is not necessary. We can be perfect on our own.

POISED TO BE SHATTERED

This idea both Augustine and the church rejected emphatically. We are sinners who cannot overcome our sin by ourselves. It is because of sin and its severity that we need a Savior. We need someone who will save us from the wrath to come.

Our best works are not good enough to meet God's standard of righteousness. Augustine defined our finest efforts as but "splendid vices." We flatter ourselves on our performance because we judge ourselves on a curve. We compare ourselves with others, and as long as there are people who seem more sinful than us, we congratulate ourselves on our virtue. This is folly, as the apostle Paul indicates:

> For we dare not class ourselves or compare ourselves with those who commend themselves. But they, measuring themselves by themselves, and comparing themselves among themselves, are not wise. We, however, will not boast beyond measure, but within the limits of the sphere which God appointed us (2 Corinthians 10:12-13a).

As long as we commit the folly of judging ourselves by ourselves or judging ourselves among ourselves, we will remain brittle in our self-esteem. We are poised to be shattered. For when we glimpse the holy character of God as the true standard, we will be like so many Humpty Dumptys. We will have such a radical fall that all the king's horses and all the king's men will not be able to repair the damage.

Our damaged souls need more than earthly royalty to rescue us from the wrath of God. We need a greater remedy. We need an atonement. We need the cross.

PART II

Saved *by* What?

3

Saved *by* What?

WE HAVE SEEN THAT the grand paradox or supreme irony of the Christian faith is that we are saved both *by* God and *from* God. The God of perfect holiness, who demands satisfaction for His justice and who will not wink at sin, has from all eternity decreed that He Himself should provide salvation to those very people who, by their sin, are exposed to His wrath and judgment.

The means *by* which God accomplishes this great salvation may be described as the most crucial aspect of the work of Christ. Indeed, His work goes to the crux of the matter. In these past two sentences I deliberately used two English words that come directly from the Latin word for cross (*crux*). The words *crucial, crux,* and also *excruciating,* all derive from this word.

BRANDS AND LOGOS

I am regularly amazed at the effort exerted by Madison Avenue advertising executives. It has become a nonnegotiable axiom in American business that "it pays to advertise." I may dispute that claim, but while I'm disputing it, I am doing so clad in an advertised shirt, an advertised pair of slacks, and advertised shoes. I am using an advertised pen to write these words in a place to which I drove in an advertised car.

Businessmen scramble to increase their market share. They are deeply concerned with name recognition in the marketplace. Billions of dollars are spent every year in this endeavor as graphic designers are enlisted to create and enhance logos, those little emblems, images, or pictures that identify or brand a particular product or company. People actually steal the hood ornaments from Mercedes automobiles so they can own at least the symbol of the luxury car if they can't buy the car itself.

It has been said that the most recognizable logo in the United States of America is a funny-looking shape that resembles a bow tie. It is found on a particular brand of automobile that is linked with motherhood and apple pie in our national folklore. The "bow tie" is the logo of Chevrolet.

Turning our attention away from business and to the realm of faith, we see that the universal symbol of Christianity is the cross. The cross crystallizes the essence of the ministry of Jesus. It captures the deepest dimension of His grand passion. So central to Christianity is the cross that Paul, engaging in a bit of hyperbole, said that he was determined to preach nothing but Christ and Him crucified (1 Corinthians 2:2). Using words instead of oil paint or a chisel and stone, Paul employs a technique that was later called the "fruitful moment" by great artists. Rembrandt and Michelangelo would sketch scores of scenes from the lives of their subjects before choosing one to memorialize in their art. For example, Michelangelo sought to capture the essence of David in one specific pose. For Paul, the fruitful moment in the life and ministry of Jesus was the cross. In a sense all of Paul's writing was simply further commentary on this defining act, that ministry in which Jesus met His hour, the ministry for which He was born and for which He was baptized. This was the ministry Jesus was preordained to carry out. He moved inexorably toward the moment that theology calls the grand passion of Christ, before which He sweat drops of blood. Everything in the life of Jesus converged in the point of climax of His death.

If we were able to read the New Testament for the first time, as if we were the first generation of people to hear the message, I think that it would be crystal clear that this event—the crucifixion of Christ, along with His resurrection and ascension—was at the very core of the preaching, teaching, and catechizing of the New Testament community. If it is true that the cross is of central and not peripheral importance to biblical Christianity, it is essential that Christians have some understanding of its meaning in biblical terms. That would be true in any generation, but I think it is particularly necessary in this generation.

THE SIGNIFICANCE OF THE CROSS

I doubt that there has ever been a time in the two thousand years of Christian history when the significance of the cross, the centrality of the cross, and the question of the necessity of the cross has been such a controversial matter as it is right now. Never before in Christian history has the need for atonement been as widely challenged as it is today. From a historical perspective there have been other times in church history when theologies emerged that regarded the cross of Christ as an unnecessary event. These theologies declared that it had value, to be sure, but that it was not something that people needed in any ultimate or significant way.

I find it interesting how so many people explain to me that the reason they are not Christians is not so much that they dispute the truth claims of Christianity, but rather that they have never been persuaded of the need for Christ. How many times have you spoken with people who have said, "It may or may not be true, but I personally don't feel the need for Jesus," or, "I don't need the church," or, "I don't need Christianity"? When I hear comments like this, my spirit groans within me. I tremble to think of the consequences if people persist in such an attitude. If we could persuade people of the identity of Christ and the truth of His work, it would become instantly apparent that every person in the world needs it and that without it there would be no salvation *from* God.

While in a shopping mall not long ago, I wandered into a large bookstore. It was a secular bookstore with rack after rack of books for sale. Various divisions of the bookstore were marked prominently with labels such as "fiction," "non-fiction," "business," "sports," "self-improvement," "sex and marriage," and so forth. All the way back in the rear of the store there was a section on religion. This section had about four shelves. It was the smallest section in the store. The material on those racks was hardly compatible with orthodox, classical Christianity. I asked myself, "What's wrong with this store that all they sell is fiction and self-improvement, and they don't seem to place any value on the content of biblical truth?" Then I remembered that the storeowners are not there as a ministry. They are there for business. They are there to make a profit. The reason they don't have many Christian books for sale is that there are not many people who come in and ask, "Where can I find a book that will teach me about the depths and the riches of the atonement of Christ?"

Then I thought, *Perhaps if I go to a Christian bookstore, I'll find such an emphasis.* But no, Christian bookstores offer precious little literature on the cross of Christ. I thought about that while sitting in the mall and watching people walk back and forth in front of me. I got an impression. It was a scary impression that these masses of people walking back and forth were not concerned about an atonement for sin because they were basically convinced that they had no need for such an atonement. Such an atonement is simply not a "felt need" for people today. People are not pressed by the question, "How can I be reconciled to God? How can I escape the judgment of God?"

One thing that indisputably has been lost from our culture is the idea that human beings are privately, personally, inexorably accountable to God for their lives. Imagine what would happen if suddenly the lights came on and everyone in the world said, "Hey, someday I will stand before my Maker, and I will have to give an account for every word that I have spoken, every deed that I have done, every thought that I have thought, and every task that I have failed to do. I am accountable."

If everyone were to wake up to that fact instantly, a couple of things could happen. People could say, "Well, yes, I'm accountable, but isn't it great that the One to whom and before whom I am accountable isn't really concerned about what kind of a life I lead, because He understands that boys will be boys and that girls will be girls?" If everyone were to say something like that, maybe nothing would change. But if people understood two things—if they understood that God is holy and that sin is an offense against His holiness—then they would be breaking down the doors of our churches, pleading, "What must I do to be saved?"

We may like to think that we don't need a Savior, but the atonement and the cross and Christianity operate on the primary assumption that we are in desperate need of salvation. That assumption may not be shared by our modern culture, but that does not lessen the reality of the need.

I'm afraid that in the United States of America today the prevailing doctrine of justification is not justification by faith alone. It is not even justification by good works or by a combination of faith and works. The prevailing notion of justification in our culture today is justification by death. All one has to do to be received into the everlasting arms of God is to die. That is all that's required. Death somehow erases our sin—an atonement is not necessary.

A theologian friend of mine says frequently that in church history there have been only three basic types of theology. There have been a multitude of theological schools with subtle nuances, but in the final analysis there are only three kinds of theology: what we call Pelagianism, semi-Pelagianism, and Augustinianism. Virtually every church in Western church history, and in Eastern church history as well, has fallen into one of those three categories. Semi-Pelagianism and Augustinianism represent significant debates within the Christian family—differences of opinion on biblical interpretation and theology among Christians. But Pelagianism in its various forms does not involve mere intramural issues among Christians. Pelagianism is at best sub-Christian and at worst anti-Christian. Pelagianism in the fourth century, Socinianism in the sixteenth and seventeenth centuries, and what we would call liberalism as a distinctive theology today are essentially non-Christian because at the heart of these views is a denial of the atonement of Jesus Christ—a denial of the cross as an act of satisfying God's justice. For centuries, orthodox Christianity has seen the atonement as a *sine qua non* of the Christian faith. Take away the cross as an atoning act, and you take away Christianity.

It is not as if the Pelagians, the Socinians, and liberalism have no view of the significance of the cross of Christ. They declare that the cross shows Jesus dying as a moral example for mankind—as an existential hero, as One who brings inspiration to us by His commitment and devotion to self-sacrifice and humanistic concerns. But these examples of morality fall short of atonement.

When I was in seminary, one of my classmates gave a sermon in homiletics class on the cross of Christ as the Lamb slain for us. When he was finished, the professor was furious. He verbally attacked the student while he was still standing in the pulpit. He said in his rage, "How dare you preach a substitutionary view of the atonement in this day and age?" He saw the substitutionary view of the atonement as an archaic, old-fashioned notion of one person dying to bear the sins of others. He categorically rejected the cross as a kind of cosmic transaction by which we are reconciled to God.

But if we take away the reconciling action of Christ from the New Testament, we are left with nothing but moralisms that are anything but unique and are hardly worth persuading people to give their lives for. In Pelagianism and liberalism there is no salvation. In Pelagianism and liberalism there is no Savior, because in Pelagianism and liberalism there is no conviction that salvation is necessary.

THE NECESSITY OF THE CROSS

I have said there are three basic types of theology. There are also three basic views of the atonement with respect to *necessity* historically. There are those like the Socinians and Pelagians who have believed that an atonement is absolutely unnecessary. Then there are those who believe an atonement is only *hypothetically* necessary.

Now to understand that, we have to stop for a second and proceed slowly. The "hypothetical" necessity of atonement refers to the idea that God could have redeemed us by many different means, but He chose to redeem us by the cross. The method He chose was by atonement, but He could have done it many different ways. He could simply have chosen to overlook human sin, but He decided to do something dramatic, and He committed Himself to a certain course of action. Once He committed Himself, and determined to have an atonement, then it became necessary, but only necessary *de pacto*—that is, by virtue of a pact or covenant He had made, a promise that He would do something in a certain way. The promise was gratuitous. There was no need for it. But He made the promise. And once He had made the promise, then He committed Himself to that course of action. That's what is meant by a hypothetical necessity for an atonement.

The third view, which is the orthodox Christian view and, I am persuaded, the biblical view, is that an atonement was not merely hypothetically necessary for man's redemption but was absolutely necessary.

Why is an atonement necessary? I will address this question in the next chapter. But by way of preview, let me say that the heart of the issue all the way back to Pelagianism has to do with our understanding of the nature and character of God, and the nature of sin. If we are defective in our understanding of the character of God or in our understanding of the nature of sin, it is inevitable that we will come to the conclusion that an atonement is not necessary.

Again, by way of preview, let me just say three things about the character of sin from a biblical perspective. There are three distinct ways in which human sin is described biblically. First, it is described as a debt, a failure to do what we are obligated to do. God as Creator has given us responsibilities for which He holds us accountable. If we do not carry out those responsibilities, we incur a debt. Secondly, sin from the biblical perspective is an expression of enmity—a violation of the personal relationship that human beings are supposed to have with their Creator. When we sin against God, we break that relationship. We communicate not love or affection or devotion to our Creator, but a kind of hostility that has to be dealt with. And thirdly, the Bible regards sin as a crime against God, an offense against His holiness, a transgression of His Law.

It is important that we keep these three concepts clear in our minds as we explore what has to be done to restore the relationship between God and His fallen humanity. If a crime has been committed, then we have to deal with penal sanctions. If a debt has been incurred, then payment must be made. If enmity has entered a personal relationship, if the relationship has been violated, that relationship must be restored.

4

The Drama of Redemption

AT THE CLOSE OF OUR last chapter we looked briefly at the dimensions of mankind's sin against God in order to see why an atonement is necessary. Three dimensions were stressed that make it necessary for an atonement to take place. I focused attention on this threefold need in order to develop it in some kind of symmetrical pattern. As we now focus more fully on these three aspects of our need for atonement, we will see that there are also three major actors in the drama of redemption—man, God the Father, and God the Son in His incarnate work as Messiah and Redeemer.

The three dimensions of sin that necessitate atonement are: 1) sin is a debt; 2) sin is an act of enmity; and 3) sin is a crime. To understand the debt aspect of sin, we must first understand the role of God as Creator and as Sovereign over the universe.

God's sovereignty is multifaceted. It concerns His absolute rule over nature, over history, over the affairs of mankind. Indeed, God's sovereignty focuses on His authority over all creation. Sovereignty involves authority. We see another word contained within the word *authority*. It is the word *author*. As the Author of all things, God has authority over all that He creates. As the Author of all things, He is thereby the Owner of all things. What He makes and owns He rules over. God intrinsically and absolutely has the right to impose obligations on His creation. He may and can command the light to shine and the stars to move in their courses. In our culture there is much confusion over the nature of authority. When we talk about duly constituted authority, we're talking about a person or office that has the right to impose obligation. If someone in authority over me issues a command to me that is morally sound, that person has the right to impose obligation, and I am responsible to carry out that obligation. If I fail to carry out that obligation, then I must face punitive sanctions.

That is what we are talking about when we talk about God's authority. God has the authority to impose obligations on His creatures. He demands that we obey Him. "You shall be holy; for I am holy" (Leviticus 11:44). God does not rule by referendum. He does not rule by plebiscite. He does not simply give ten suggestions or ten recommendations to Israel. He gives commandments, "Thou shalt," or, "Thou shalt not," which we call "apodictic" law—law that flows from a sense of absolute authority and sovereignty.

SIN AS DEBT

If God imposes obligations upon us that we fail to perform, then we incur debt. At this point God becomes a creditor. He is the One to whom we owe the debt. Jesus described us as debtors who cannot pay our debts. It is one thing to be in debt and to be able to pay it by means of a debt-retirement program, whereby we pay off our debt a little bit at a time. But the indebtedness that we have with respect to obedience to God is impossible for us to pay back by installment plan or any other means. Why? What is the obligation ethically that God imposes upon His creatures? How righteous are we required to be? How moral are we called to be by divine mandate? We are required to be sinless—nothing less than moral perfection is required. We are like Lady Macbeth. After she committed murder, she tried desperately to wipe away the blood from her hands, but the spot was indelible. She could not get rid of it. The problem with our obligation to God is that we are called and responsible to be perfect. But if we sin once, what can we then do to be perfect? How much interest must we pay in addition to the principle in order to make up for the blemish? What do I have to do to become perfect after I have once become imperfect? There is absolutely nothing I can do. Once a person has a single moral blemish, it is impossible to erase it. I should say, it is impossible for *us* to erase it. The good news is that God (and God only) can erase it.

> "Come now, and let us reason together,"
> Says the LORD,
> "Though your sins are like scarlet,
> They shall be as white as snow;
> Though they are red like crimson,
> They shall be as wool" (Isaiah 1:18).

In our culture we try to evade the consequences of our sin by declaring, "Everyone gets a second chance." We even promote this second chance to the level of merit by saying, "Everyone deserves a second chance." But who says anybody deserves a second chance? Does justice require that everyone get a second chance? A second chance is grace. A second chance is mercy. Mercy and grace are things that are never deserved. They cannot be deserved. If they were deserved, they would be justice and not mercy. Deserved grace is simply not grace at all. To say that the creature deserves a second chance from the Creator is pure nonsense. Even if this nonsensical notion were true, what good would it do us? How long ago did we all use up our second chance?

Our problem is not that we are almost impeccable moral creatures with one tiny blemish marring a perfect record. Rather, the Scriptures describe us as woefully inadequate in terms of our obedience to God. It is not that we are merely tainted by an occasional peccadillo. Our sins are many and grave, so grave that payback is impossible.

If somebody said to me, "Okay, R. C., your financial balance system says that you owe $10,000. We'll set up a program by which you can pay off your debts eventually," I could handle that. But what would I do if somebody said, "You owe $10 billion, and you've got three days to pay it"? Would it be possible for me to pay it? Yes, it is possible. It's possible I could come up with $10 billion in three days. The possibility exists, but the odds of my doing it are astronomically remote. This scenario fails as a true analogy because, however remote the odds are, it is still within the realm of possibility that I could pay my debt. But my ability to pay the debt I owe to God is beyond the realm of possibility. There is no way I can pay it.

How does Christ help me with my debt? What is the role that He carries out in His work as our Redeemer? The New Testament has a word for it. Christ is our "surety" (see Hebrews 7:22). "Surety" is an economic term, just as "debt" is an economic term. When the Bible speaks this way, it borrows language from the business world. That Christ is our surety means that He is the One who cosigns our note. He backs up our indebtedness by taking upon Himself the obligation to pay what must be paid.

SIN AS ENMITY

We do not disobey God because we love Him deeply. We disobey God because we have an inborn hostility toward Him. The Bible says that we are by nature enemies of God. We have a natural antipathy in our fallenness toward God's reign over us. So with respect to enmity, God is the injured or offended party. It is not that God has manifested enmity toward us. We are the ones who have violated Him. God has never broken a promise. He has never violated a covenant. He has never sworn a vow to us that He failed to pay. He has never treated a human being unjustly. He has never violated me as a creature. He has never violated you. He has kept His side of the relationship perfectly. But we have violated Him. He is the injured party, not we.

We may consider these things and deem them elementary. They are simple truths we learned in Sunday school. We skip over them lightly and skate over the depth of hostility we have by nature toward God. Multitudes of people are intensely angry with God because deep down in their bones they sense that somehow God has not given them a fair deal. "How could God allow this to happen to me?" is the complaint. The unspoken statement here is, "If God were really good, if God were really just, He would recognize my merit and treat me accordingly. He would give me more than I have. God is not fair." That is the complaint deeply lodged in our bones.

We have to understand that from a biblical perspective it is God who is the injured party, not we. "But wait a minute," we say, "God doesn't suffer. We're the ones who suffer. God doesn't have to go through the vale of sorrows that we're called to go through in this world. God has perfect felicity. He's eternally happy. We're periodically happy but for the most part miserable." So how can we talk about God's being the injured party? We can talk in such terms because God is the One who is violated, and He is perfect. He does not deserve any of this violation that we heap upon Him.

Can I ever say to God that I suffer at His hands unjustly? I may suffer at the hands of other people unjustly. We know that there is abundant injustice in this world between people, where one person steals from another, or lies to another, or cheats or harms another. On the horizontal level there are all kinds of injustices in the world.

But how much injustice passes vertically from God to man? If someone violates me and makes me a victim of his unjust activity, I may say, "God, avenge me of this, vindicate me, restore me, redeem me from this man's unjust activity toward me." But I cannot say, "God, the fact that you allowed him to commit an injustice against me is unjust on your part in terms of our vertical relationship." I can say it—but I cannot say it justly. Nothing that could ever happen to me in this world would give me a just reason to assault the integrity of God in terms of His relationship to me.

God is the injured party—not we. The role that Christ plays in our redemption is that of mediator. What does a mediator do? Where does the mediator stand? He stands in the middle, which is not a very popular place to be. In cases of estrangement, the mediator usually catches flak from both sides. It is like being an umpire or a referee between two combatants. The mediator often becomes a human lightning rod, attracting heat from both sides.

When we talk about mediation, we are concerned about *reconciliation*, a theme that is crucial to biblical Christianity. The purpose of mediation in an industrial contract dispute between labor and management is to accomplish reconciliation. The mediator is brought in to bring the two sides together where previous negotiations have failed. If there is no need for reconciliation, there is no need for a mediator. Reconciliation is needed only when estrangement has occurred—only when a relationship has been ruptured.

The Scriptures speak of such a ruptured personal relationship, a relationship that has been broken between two parties—God and man. There exists an estrangement between God and man, and reconciliation is necessary. It is into this situation of estrangement, of brokenness, that Christ comes as mediator. He is our supreme mediator. Paul writes:

> For there is one God and one Mediator between God and men, the Man Christ Jesus, who gave Himself a ransom for all (1 Timothy 2:5-6a).

The fact that Christ came to mediate a broken relationship raises the question, "Who is mad at whom here?" Who is estranged? Obviously we are estranged from God and we manifest our enmity by our continual disobedience. What about the other side? Is it proper to talk about God's being estranged from us? Is God angry with us? When I ask this question to live audiences, it is as though I am looking at stones and logs. I get no response. Does the silence mean obvious consent? I think not. People will finally respond by saying something like, "God is disappointed, but not angry." People tend to choke on the idea of any real wrath in God. But the biblical revelation indicates that God is sorely displeased with our offenses; and God the Father, as the injured party, is angry with our sin.

Though many deny the reality of God's wrath, it is taught so plainly in Scripture that others are loath to deny it. But they often fall off the other side of the horse. They substitute one distortion for the other. This error occurs when God the Father is seen as being so consumed with wrath toward us that it requires the benevolent and kind intervention of the Son to bring the Father around—God the Father is mad as a hornet at man, but God the Son identifies so closely with our fallenness and our need that in His love, patience, and compassion He sides with us and acts as our mediator to calm down the angry Father. This view posits a tension or split within the Godhead itself, as if the Father had one agenda and the Son persuaded Him to change His mind. The Father is angry and intends to mete out punishment and send everyone to hell, until the Son intervenes to talk Him out of it. This view sees Jesus saying, "Punish Me instead. Let Me stand in their place. Let Me not only mediate the discussion, but let Me absorb the anger. Pile it on Me, not on them. Let Me be the lightning rod, and You can take Your wrath out on Me."

This may seem to be a ridiculous scenario, but it reflects a serious objection raised by sophisticated theologians at a very technical level. And it is a widespread, prevalent picture among "ordinary" Christians as well. I have wondered frequently why evangelical Christians tend to be "unitarians" focusing almost exclusively on the Second Person of the Trinity. Why is there so much warm passion, love, and affection for Jesus, while the Father is almost totally ignored in Christian study, devotion, and liturgy? How can that be? Maybe there's a sense that, "Okay, Jesus we can relate to, but the Father? That's another matter. We still have to be wary of the Father because He's the angry One." However, when we think like this, we forget whose idea it was to provide a mediator in the first place. The Mediator did not come on His own. God so loved the world that He "gave," that He "sent" His Son. Those two verbs we find in the Bible again and again and again. The Father sends the Son. The Father gives the Son for our redemption:

> For it pleased the Father that in Him all the fullness should dwell, and by Him to reconcile all things to Himself, by Him, whether things on earth or things in heaven, having made peace through the blood of His cross. And you, who once were alienated and enemies in your mind by wicked works, yet now He has reconciled in the body of His flesh through death, to present you holy, and blameless, and above reproach in His sight (Colossians 1:19-22).

SIN AS CRIME

The third dimension of sin is its criminal characteristic. Here God functions as the Governor and the Judge. God is ultimately the Judge in all matters of justice. He is the ultimate standard of righteousness. His own character is the ultimate standard of justice. He functions personally as the Judge of heaven and earth. Christ in the drama of the atonement does not function as the Judge. He is elevated to the role of Judge in His ascension, however, and that is very significant. By contrast, in His descent to this world, Christ comes under judgment, and His role here is as priest-victim. He comes to be judged in our behalf.

At this point we must grasp the important difference between a simple debt and a crime. They do have something in common. A crime is actually a kind of debt. It is a moral debt. In historical theology a distinction is made between two types of debt: a pecuniary (or monetary) debt and a penal (moral) debt. The difference between a pecuniary debt and a moral debt may be seen in the following illustration.

Suppose I enter an ice-cream parlor and watch a small boy order an ice-cream cone with two scoops. The woman behind the counter prepares the cone and says to the boy, "That will be $2.00."

The child becomes crestfallen and replies, "But my mommy only gave me a dollar."

What would I do if I witnessed this? I would do what I guess any compassionate adult would do. I would reach into my pocket, pull out a dollar, and give it to the lady to make up for the pecuniary shortfall. When I hand over the dollar, I am handing over legal tender. The woman must accept the payment for the boy's cone. The monetary debt is paid in full, and the boy no longer owes the woman anything.

But suppose the scenario unfolds in a different manner. Suppose the woman hands the cone to the boy and says, "That will be $2.00," whereupon the boy turns and runs out the door, cone in hand, without paying anything. Sadly for him, he runs right into a policeman, who marches him back into the store.

Now I say, "It's okay. I'll pay what he owes. Let him go." At this point, must the storeowner or the policeman let the boy go? By no means. By running out of the store, the boy committed an act of theft. He committed a crime. His problem has been elevated from a monetary debt to a moral debt. In addition to the financial dimension, a crime has been committed, a violation of justice has taken place, a person has been wronged. Now who is the only person who has the right to decide whether or not to accept my money as payment in full on behalf of the boy? The one who has been violated. If the storeowner decides not to press charges, the boy may go free. But there is no requirement, either legally or morally, for the store owner not to press charges. Such a decision would be an act of grace.

When I sin against God, Jesus pays the price for my indebtedness. In order for that payment to be accepted, the Judge, who is at the same time the injured party, must decide and decree that He will accept that payment in my behalf. If I owed God the death penalty because I sinned against Him, and Jesus said, "I will die for him," and laid down His life for me, would God be under any obligation whatsoever to accept that payment? None whatsoever. There first must be a decision by the Governor of the universe that He will accept a substitutionary payment in order for my crime to be covered. The decision of God the Father to do so is one of sheer grace.

God demands that justice be done. The price must be paid. The debt will be paid in full, in both a pecuniary sense and a penal sense. He judges our crime. Our crime is punished. The debt is paid. God does not negotiate His justice. Yet at the same time our debt and the punishment for our crime are paid by a Substitute. Thus the cross shows both perfect justice and perfect mercy. Take away the substitution and you take away the grace of God. Take away the cross and you take away the justice and righteousness of God. In this transaction we see what Paul meant when he said that God is "just and the justifier of the one who has faith in Jesus" (Romans 3:26).

Law Justice | Grace

By law we are guilty and must pay the penalty unless Father agrees to forgive. He agreed to accept a substitute (Jesus) to pay the penalty (death) in our place thus allowing us to be set free. We do not deserve it as we are totally guilty. By grace + mercy Christ took our place.

5

Christ Our Ransom

I'M SURE THERE WERE times in Jesus' ministry, particularly toward the end, when He had to be frustrated with His disciples. When He made His last trip from Galilee down to Jerusalem, He focused attention on His coming hour and prepared His disciples for His death in the Holy City. Somehow it didn't get across to them. They struggled with the words Jesus spoke to them. In Mark's Gospel we read:

> Now they were on the road, going up to Jerusalem, and Jesus was going before them; and they were amazed. And as they followed they were afraid. Then He took the twelve aside again and began to tell them the things that would happen to Him: "Behold, we are going up to Jerusalem, and the Son of Man will be betrayed to the chief priests and to the scribes; and they will condemn Him to death and deliver Him to the Gentiles; and they will mock Him, and scourge Him, and spit on Him, and kill Him. And the third day He will rise again" (10:32-34).

Within moments the disciples changed the topic and began arguing about which of them would sit at Jesus' right hand in

His kingdom. Christ was preparing to enter into His grand passion, and His closest friends were already arguing about their inheritance. It was in this context that Jesus said something very significant for our understanding of the atonement:

> "You know that those who are considered rulers over the Gentiles lord it over them, and their great ones exercise authority over them. Yet it shall not be so among you; but whoever desires to become great among you shall be your servant. And whoever of you desires to be first shall be slave of all. For even the Son of Man did not come to be served, but to serve, and to give His life a ransom for many" (Mark 10:42-45).

When Jesus had to state succinctly, poignantly, and graphically what His ministry was about so that His disciples would understand, He framed His mission in terms of giving His life as a ransom.

The concept of *ransom* is the root concept in the New Testament behind the broader term *redemption.* In biblical categories a redeemer is one who provides a ransom. The Greek word here translated "ransom" is *lutron.*

One of the first words learned in elementary Greek is the verb *luo,* which means to "loose," to "set free," to "unbind." The concept of ransom is built upon this root of loosing something, setting something free that is held in captivity. In the ancient world the idea of ransom functioned very much like the idea of ransom in our own language. When we think of ransom, we think of kidnapping, where someone abducts a person and then demands payment for the release of the person who is being held hostage. The kidnappers expect a monetary payment. That is similar to how the concept functioned in antiquity. The ransom was a price paid to release a slave from bondage. Or hostages held in military conflicts could be purchased and set free by a ransom.

Who set the price tag for the ransom? It was not established by some board of trade that came in and figured out the going market rate. The price tag for the ransom was set initially by the slaveholder or the hostage holder. He determined the ransom price, and then let the person who was trying to free the hostage, slave, or kidnapped person decide if the price was too high.

Many theories about the atonement have been set forth. Part of the reason for the multitude of theories is that the Bible itself describes the cross as a multifaceted event. Various images are used to describe it. There are different aspects of salvation taking place, all converging in this one moment of redemptive history. One of the images used in the New Testament to describe this multifaceted event is this image of ransom—a ransom paid to redeem a captive. That is what redemption is all about—being set free. Similarly, Old Testament Israel was redeemed. God was the Redeemer when He delivered His people from bondage in Egypt. The Exodus is a story about redemption.

One of the theories of the atonement that has competed for acceptance throughout church history—the so-called ransom theory—is that in the transaction of the cross Jesus pays a ransom to Satan, because Satan has bound man and held him captive. Satan holds mankind in chains and is like a kidnapper who snatches us away from our Father's house. Christ comes and pays the ransom to set us free.

In passing, let me add that another element clearly present in the biblical view of the atonement is what has been called the *Christus Victor* element. This calls attention to the aspect of Christ's work by which He achieved a cosmic victory over the demonic principalities and powers. He came to destroy the work of the devil, to conquer Satan and his power over us.

I do not want to minimize in any way that the New Testament has a strong victory motif. Christ conquers the demonic forces, the forces of Satan that are hostile toward us. We see that antithesis and the titanic struggle that went on from the very beginning of Jesus' ministry when the Spirit led Him into the wilderness to be tempted of Satan. When He withstood that temptation, we read, almost as a postscript, that Satan departed from Him "for a season." The retreat of Satan was not a permanent retreat. It was what we would call strategic withdrawal, so that he could find a better place to launch another assault against Christ. The conflict permeated the ministry of Jesus. And the Bible says that in His death, Christ conquered Satan.

Yes, there is clearly that element of the struggle between Christ and the principalities and powers of Satan. But that does not mean that the ransom of which Christ speaks is paid to Satan. Think of it for a moment. If Christ paid a ransom to Satan to deliver you from Satan's clutches, who would the victor be? The kidnapper does not want permanent possession of the child. He wants what the child can get for him through extortion and through a premium ransom. If he can get the distraught parents to pay the ransom, he wins.

If the ransom is paid to Satan, Satan laughs all the way to the bank. And there is no *Christus Victor*. Rather, there is

Satanus Victor. But when the Bible speaks of ransom, the ransom is paid not to a criminal but to the One who is owed the price for redemption—the One who is the offended party, the injured party in the whole process of sin. And who is that? Again, it is God the Father. Jesus, as the Servant, offers Himself in payment to the Father for us.

SUBSTITUTION AND SATISFACTION

Even critical scholars who reject the biblical view of atonement will often admit that the Scriptures portray the atonement as involving two indisputable elements: *substitution* and *satisfaction.* The fact that the New Testament writers understood Jesus' ministry on the cross in terms of a ransom demands an understanding of substitution and satisfaction. In a ransom situation, a price is paid by someone other than the individual *for* whom it is being paid. The demand for the ransom is being *satisfied* by a *substitute.* Karl Barth once waxed eloquent saying that the single most important Greek word in all of the New Testament is a tiny little word *huper,* which is translated by three English words, "in behalf of." "I lay down my life for my sheep"—"in behalf of" my sheep. "I give my life in behalf of the many." In behalf of, in behalf of, in behalf of—this is the recurring, resounding refrain of Jesus' own self-understanding.

When we see a painting in a museum, we may scratch our heads and muse, "I wonder what the artist meant by this." We can speculate forever about what was in his mind when he painted it, what his intended meaning was. But the question can be answered in an instant if we can ask the artist himself about it. Sometimes artists are evasive and reply, "I painted it—it's up to you to interpret it. It means whatever you think it means."

That is how an existential artist may respond—by fleeing into pure subjectivism.

Fortunately Jesus was not an existentialist. When Jesus explained His agenda, He was talking in the first person and communicating to His hearers what His mission was. At the center of His teaching was this: He was not working to save Himself; He was offering Himself as a substitute in our behalf.

EXPIATION AND PROPITIATION

When we talk technically about the atonement, two words come up repeatedly. These two words often provoke consternation and debate. The words are "expiation" and "propitiation."

We know from the prefix *ex* ("out of" or "from") that the word *expiation* means to remove something or to take something away. In biblical terms it has to do with taking away guilt, removing guilt by way of paying a ransom or offering an atonement; it has to do with paying the penalty for something. So the act of expiation removes the problem by paying for it, either by paying a penalty, paying a ransom, or making a sacrifice in order to satisfy some demand. Propitiation, by contrast, has to do with the object of the expiation. The cue to remembering this is the prefixes. *Ex* means "away from" or "out of." *Pro* usually means "for" or "in front of."

Propitiation has to do with that which brings about a change in God's attitude, when we are restored into fellowship and into favor with God. There is a sense in which we can talk here of God's being appeased. We know how the word *appeasement* functions in military and political conflicts. We think of the so-called politics of appeasement, that if you have a rambunctious world conqueror on the loose rattling the sword, rather than risk the wrath of his blitzkrieg you give him Czechoslovakia or Poland. You try to assuage his wrath and appease him by giving him something that will satisfy him so that he won't come into your country and mow you down. That's an ungodly manifestation of appeasement.

The same Greek word (*hilasmos*) can be translated either as "expiation" or as "propitiation." But there is an important difference in the terms. Expiation is the act that results in the change of God's disposition toward us. Expiation is what Christ does on the cross. The result of Christ's work of expiation is that God is propitiated. And the bottom-line result is that we are then reconciled. This would be the distinction between the ransom that is paid and the attitude of the one who receives the ransom.

The one element that is involved in both expiation and propitiation is an act of placation. The work of Christ was done to placate the wrath of God. This idea of placating the wrath of God has done little to placate the wrath of modern theologians. Modern theologians have become wrathful about the idea of placating the wrath of God! They think that it is beneath the dignity of God that He has to be placated—that we have to do something to soothe Him or to appease Him. I grant that we need to be very careful in how we understand the wrath of God and placation. But let me remind you that the concept of placating the wrath of God has to do not with a peripheral, tangential point of theology, but with the very essence of salvation.

When we talk about salvation biblically, we have to remember from what ultimately we are saved. We are saved from the wrath that is to come, the wrath of God. We cannot understand either the mission of Christ or His cross apart from Jesus' own teaching about judgment. He constantly warned people that someday the whole world was coming into judgment. What is done in corners and in secret will be made manifest. Jesus said that every idle word will come into the judgment. His was a "crisis" theology. The Greek word *krisis* means "judgment." The crisis of which Jesus preached was the crisis of an impending judgment of the world, at which point God is going to pour out His wrath against the unredeemed, the ungodly, and the impenitent. The only hope of escape from the wrath of God is to be covered by the atonement of Christ. The supreme achievement of the cross is that Christ has placated the wrath of God, which would burn against me were I not covered by His sacrifice.

6

Blessing or Curse?

WHEN WE CONSIDER THE cross of Christ, we see an event in history that stands out with so much importance and significance that it is easy to overlook that the cross was not an isolated event in history that sprung up spontaneously. Rather, the atonement of Christ was the culmination, the climax of centuries of redemptive history. Ages and ages before, God had set certain things in motion that reached their acme with the death of Jesus.

ATONEMENT AND COVENANT

Coming from the Reformation tradition, I am greatly concerned that we understand the work of Christ in the atonement within the broader framework of what is called the "covenant." It is impossible to fully understand the death of Christ apart from an understanding of the whole process of covenant that is worked out in the Old and New Testaments.

For example, when Jesus went to the Upper Room the night before He was crucified, He was acutely conscious of participating in a covenant rite. He told His disciples that He had a deep desire to celebrate the Passover with them. He made painstaking preparations to meet with them in the Upper Room to celebrate the central ceremony and "sacrament" of the old covenant. While taking part in that process, He gave new meaning to the old signs. He instituted a new covenant with the breaking of bread and the drinking of wine and by saying, "This is My body broken for you," with respect to the bread. With respect to the cup He said, "This is the blood of the new covenant, which is shed for the remission of sins." Suddenly the symbol of the wine no longer referred simply to the Passover event where the blood of the lamb was spread upon the doorposts so that the angel of death would pass over the children of Israel. Now the wine was given a new sacramental meaning pointing to the blood that was to be shed by Christ in His atoning death. In Christ's Upper Room conversation, covenantal language abounded.

To get a glimpse of one vital element of the atonement, we must look back to the Old Testament book of Deuteronomy. Here some of the terms of the covenant that God made with the people of Israel are spelled out. If we study the elements of covenants in the ancient world, we see that though the content of covenants may differ from culture to culture, there were certain elements and aspects of a covenant that were virtually universal. Whenever a legal agreement like this was entered into, the sovereign party in the covenant would identify himself and would rehearse the history of his relationship to the subordinates in the covenant. This was true among the Sumerians and the Hittites and other peoples of antiquity as well as the Jews.

When God entered into covenant, He would identify Himself. He said, "I am Yahweh. I am the LORD your God who brought you out of the land of Egypt" (Deuteronomy 5:6). He gave a historical prologue before the terms of the covenant were set forth.

The terms of the covenant are called its "stipulations." Any covenant has stipulations. When we get married, we enter into a covenant. We promise to do certain things—to love, honor, obey, and so on. When we sign an industrial contract with an employer, we agree to work a certain number of hours a day. The employer agrees to provide compensation and benefits. These benefits are tied to the meeting of specific requirements. That is, for the benefits to accrue, the work must be done according to the agreement.

COVENANT BLESSINGS AND CURSES

In the ancient world every covenant had sanctions. These sanctions were usually twofold. They involved both rewards and penalties. Rewards were given for keeping the terms and stipulations of the agreement. Penalties were suffered if the terms of the agreement were violated. In the Old Testament the reward for keeping the covenant was called a "blessing." The penalty for violating the contract was called a "curse."

Deuteronomy 28 spells out the terms of the covenant that God made with the people of Israel:

> "Now it shall come to pass, if you diligently obey the voice of the LORD your God, to observe carefully all His commandments which I command you today, that the LORD your God will set you high above all nations of the earth. And all these blessings shall come upon you and overtake you, because you obey the voice of the LORD your God" (Deuteronomy 28:1-2).

The promises proceed almost as a litany. "You will be blessed in the city and blessed in the country. The fruit of your womb will be blessed, and the crops of your land and the young of your livestock—the calves of your herd and the lambs of your flocks. Your basket and your kneading trough will be blessed. You will be blessed when you come in and blessed when you go out" (see vv. 3-6, NIV).

If the terms are kept, if the commandments are obeyed, then God promises: I will bless you when you stand up, I will bless you when you sit down, I will bless you when you roll over, I will bless you when you are silent, I will bless you when you speak, I will bless you when you are in the city, I will bless you when you are in the country, I will bless you when you are on the highway, I will bless you when you are on the seas. Everywhere you go, in everything you do, you will get blessed.

Then we turn the page. After the wonderful promises of blessing are given, we encounter an ominous "However." "However, if you do not obey the LORD your God and do not carefully follow all his commands and decrees I am giving you today, all these curses will come upon you and overtake you: You will be cursed in the city and cursed in the country. Your basket and your kneading trough will be cursed. The fruit of your womb will be cursed, and the crops of your land, the calves of your herds and the lambs of your flocks. You will be cursed when you come in and cursed when you go out" (vv. 15-19, NIV).

We see a parallel here—but it is a parallel of antithesis where the curse stands in direct opposition to the blessing. If we disobey, when we stand up we will be cursed, when we sit down we will be cursed, when we go into the city we will be cursed, in the country we will be cursed, on the sea we will be cursed. Our children will be cursed, our sheep will be cursed, our dogs will be cursed, our cat will be cursed, our baker will be cursed. Note the far-ranging extent of the curse of God. It extends over all of life.

BLESSED: IN THE PRESENCE OF GOD

To grasp these sanctions we must first understand how the Jew understood the meaning of the term *blessing.* Translators of the Bible face this question when they come to the Beatitudes of Jesus. Some render the Greek by the English word *happy* ("Happy are the poor in spirit"). I fear that in their zeal to modernize the text by using language with which the public is familiar, by "correcting" archaic expressions, the profound concept of blessedness is supplanted by a shallow substitute. There is a special theological significance to the word *blessed* that is not connoted by the English word *happy.* If we translate with the word *happy,* we are impoverishing the content.

To the Jew, blessedness was to receive the supreme favor that one could possibly hope for from the hand of God. My favorite way of explaining this is to examine the classic Hebrew benediction:

> "The LORD bless you and keep you;
> The LORD make His face shine upon you,
> And be gracious to you;
> The LORD lift up His countenance upon you
> And give you peace" (Numbers 6:24-26).

Notice the poetic structure and rhythm in this benediction. We have here a Hebrew literary device called parallelism. There are different kinds of parallelism. In this benediction we have two forms of parallelism at work. First, the benediction contains three statements, each of which has two parts. The first statement says: "The LORD bless you and keep you." Two things are entreated, that one be blessed by God and kept by Him. To be kept by God is to be preserved by His benevolent providence. The history of the Jewish people was, and continues to be, a history of volatility. Rarely have they enjoyed any lasting peace as a nation. In the ancient world this tiny country formed the land bridge between Africa and Asia and Europe. It was the proverbial political football being tossed about by major world powers. The yearning for stability, for permanence, was deeply rooted in the Jewish heart. To be preserved, maintained, and sustained for a considerable period of continuity was at the core of the benediction prayer.

Second, the benediction in its three verses forms an example of synonymous parallelism. All three verses mean essentially the same thing. We have the same message stated with different words for poetic richness and diversity. I call your attention to this because the first verse contains the statement, "The LORD bless you," then clues as to how the Jew understood blessedness can be found in the next two verses: that the face of God will shine upon you; that God will lift up the light of His countenance upon you. The supreme level of blessedness would be to be able to look God in the face. From a look at other Old Testament passages, we see that blessedness had to do in the Jewish mind with proximity to the presence of God. The closer one gets to the immediate presence of God, the greater the blessedness. The further removed one is from the face of God, the less the blessedness.

The curse of God is the exact opposite of the blessing. If we turned the classic benediction into a malediction, it would go something like this: "May the Lord curse you and destroy you. May the Lord turn His back upon you and be judgmental toward you. May the Lord turn off the lights of His countenance and leave you in darkness and give you turmoil." That would be the curse of the covenant rather than the blessedness of the covenant.

In summary, for the Jew, to be blessed was to have God draw near. Our culture experienced a taste of this during the Civil Rights Movement. One of the popular songs of this movement was "We Shall Not Be Moved." The words of this song came from Psalm 46:

> God is our refuge and strength,
> A very present help in trouble.
> Therefore we will not fear,
> Even though the earth be removed,
> And though the mountains be carried into the midst of the sea;
> Though its waters roar and be troubled,
> Though the mountains shake with its swelling.
> There is a river whose streams shall make glad the city of God,
> The holy place of the tabernacle of the Most High.
> God is in the midst of her, she shall not be moved;
> God shall help her, just at the break of dawn.
> The nations raged, the kingdoms were moved;
> He uttered His voice, the earth melted.
> The LORD of hosts is with us;
> The God of Jacob is our refuge (vv. 1-7).

The psalm describes a time of crisis, a time of tumult and upheaval. It is a frightening time. Yet in the midst of surrounding calamity, confidence is found in the assurance of the presence of God. It is because God is in the midst of His people that they shall not be moved. The image of God in the presence of His people was rooted in the arrangement of the tents of the tribes in their wilderness experience. When the people of Israel would encamp in the wilderness, they were to pitch their tents according to a pattern that God gave them. The tribes would camp in a circle. In the exact center of the encampment was the tabernacle or "the tent of God's presence." God's tent was pitched in the middle, in the midst of the people, saying as it were, "Here I am."

CURSED: CUT OFF FROM GOD'S PRESENCE

Though the people of God celebrate the presence of God and the blessedness that entails, there are no hymns that celebrate His divine curse. The curse involves being cut off from the presence of God, being driven into the outer darkness, far removed from the light of His countenance. The outer darkness was the abode of the Gentile. It was "outside the camp"; it was territory occupied by those who were strangers to the covenant, by those deemed "unclean." These people were aliens or foreigners to the household of Israel.

The rituals enacted in the Old Testament ceremony of the Day of Atonement graphically signified these things. Most people are aware that on the Day of Atonement animals were sacrificed on the altar as blood offerings. But there was one animal involved in this drama of redemption that was not sacrificed on the altar. This was the scapegoat:

"And when he has made an end of atoning for the Holy Place, the tabernacle of meeting, and the altar, he shall bring the live goat. Aaron shall lay both his hands on the head of the live goat, confess over it all the iniquities of the children of Israel, and all their transgressions, concerning all their sins, putting them on the head of the goat, and shall send it away into the wilderness by the hand of a suitable man. The goat shall bear on itself all their iniquities to an uninhabited land; and he shall release the goat in the wilderness" (Leviticus 16:20-22).

In this ceremony the sins of the people were symbolically transferred to the goat's back. But the goat was not killed. Instead the goat was sent outside the camp. He was driven into the wilderness, into the place of darkness, to the place that was removed from the light of God's countenance. In effect the goat, bearing the sins of the people that had been imputed to it, was sent into the place of the curse, outside the realm of divine blessing.

JESUS OUR CURSE

When we turn our attention to the New Testament, we read an extraordinary statement from the apostle Paul with respect to the cross of Christ:

Therefore He who supplies the Spirit to you and works miracles among you, does He do it by the works of the law, or by the hearing of faith? —just as Abraham "believed God, and it was accounted to him for righteousness." Therefore know that only those who are of faith are sons of Abraham. And the Scripture, foreseeing that God would justify the Gentiles by faith, preached the gospel to Abraham beforehand, saying, "In you all the nations shall be blessed." So then those who are of faith are blessed with believing Abraham. For as many as are of the works of the law are under the curse; for it is written, "Cursed is everyone who does not continue in all things which are written in the book of the law, to do them." But that no one is justified by the law in the sight of God is evident, for "the just shall live by faith." Yet the law is not of faith, but "the man who does them shall live by them." Christ has redeemed us from the curse of the law, having become a curse for us (for it is written, "Cursed is everyone who hangs on a tree"), that the blessing of Abraham might come upon the Gentiles in Christ Jesus, that we might receive the promise of the Spirit through faith (Galatians 3:5-14).

Paul reminds the Galatians of the covenant that God made with Abraham. He called Abraham to be a blessing for the whole world. It is as though God said, "I am going to spread out this blessedness from the center, and I'm going to let it pour out and over all of the nations of the world. All nations will be blessed through you, so that all who have faith are blessed along with you."

In contrast to this blessedness that comes by faith, Paul says that all who rely on observing the Law as a means of salvation, all who trust in their own good works and their own performance, are under a curse. For it is written, "Cursed is everyone who does not continue to do everything written in the book of the law." Paul was thinking back to Deuteronomy. He was remembering the terms of the covenant. Any person who failed to keep every one of these laws was under the curse. Then Paul says clearly that no one is justified before God by the Law, "for the just shall live by faith." The Law is not based on faith.

The object of saving faith is Christ because He and He alone is able to remove the curse from us:

> Christ has redeemed us from the curse of the law, having become a curse for us (for it is written, "Cursed is everyone who hangs on a tree") (Galatians 3:13).

Paul says that in the cross Christ became a curse for us. He took upon Himself all the negative sanctions of the penalties of the Law. In taking this curse He even fulfilled the cryptic statement, "cursed is everyone who hangs upon a tree."

When we look at the intricacy of the drama of the events of Jesus' crucifixion, we see that some amazing things have taken place. The Old Testament prophetic utterances are fulfilled to the most minute detail. In the first instance the Bible says that the Messiah will be delivered to the Gentiles for judgment. It happened in the course of history that Jesus was put on trial during a time of Roman occupation. Though the Romans allowed a certain amount of home rule to their conquered vassals, they did not permit the death penalty to be imposed by local rulers. The Jews did not have the authority to put Christ to death. All that they could do was to meet in council and deliver Jesus to Pontius Pilate, who acted with Roman authority. Jesus was thus delivered from His own people to the Gentiles. He was delivered "outside the camp." He was given into the hands of the pagans, outside the camp where the face of God does not shine, where the light of God's countenance does not fall. Jesus was delivered into their hands for judgment. The Jews did not kill or execute by crucifixion. They executed by stoning. But the Romans executed by crucifixion. So the method of Jesus' death was "hanging upon a tree." The Old Testament curse, remember, was not upon everyone who was stoned; it was upon "everyone who hangs upon a tree."

Then we note the site of the actual execution. It was outside of Jerusalem. It was in Jerusalem that Jesus was first delivered to the Gentiles for judgment. Once He was judged and condemned to be executed, He was forcibly led by way of the Via Dolorosa outside of the walls of the city to Golgotha. Just as the scapegoat was driven outside the camp, outside of the Holy City where the presence of God was concentrated, so Jesus was sent into the outer darkness.

JESUS: CUT OFF FROM GOD FOR US

During the hours Jesus hung on the cross, an astronomical phenomenon occurred. In the middle of the afternoon it became dark. Darkness descended upon the land. In the midst of the intensity of this darkness, which may have involved a blotting out or obscuring of the sun (perhaps even a total eclipse), Jesus cried out. He screamed in agony, "My God, My God, why have You forsaken Me?" (Matthew 27:46). There have been various interpretations of these words of Christ. Albert Schweitzer concluded from this text that Jesus died in disillusionment. He expected that God would deliver Him, but in His final moments Jesus realized that God was not coming to His rescue. So He died much as does a disillusioned, tragic Shakespearean hero. Others point out that those words are quoted from Psalm 22. They argue that Jesus was simply identifying Himself with the suffering servant of Psalm 22. They say He was reciting poetry at His death. I do not doubt that the source of His words was that psalm, and that Jesus was aware of it. I'm sure He had read that psalm many times. But I think more was involved than His identification with the psalm.

My ordination hymn was "'Tis midnight, and on Olive's Brow." I love that hymn in spite of a line in it that bothers me. It declares that Jesus was "not forsaken by His God." Some theologians say, "Jesus, in His humanity, felt forsaken on the cross, but He wasn't really forsaken." But if Jesus was not really forsaken on the cross, we are still in our sins. We have no redemption. We have no salvation. The whole point of the cross is that if Jesus was going to bear our sins and the sanctions of the covenant, then He had to experience the fullness of the curse. He had to experience utter and complete forsakenness by the Father.

The sign of the old covenant was circumcision. In one sense it was a primitive and obscene sign. Why did the Jew cut off the foreskin of his flesh? This rite had two meanings—a positive and a negative meaning—representing the two sanctions of the covenant. The positive meaning of cutting the foreskin was that God was cutting out this group of people from the rest, separating them, setting them apart to be a holy nation, to be a blessing. The negative was that the Jew was saying, "Oh, God, if I fail to keep every one of the terms of this covenant, may I be cut off from You, cut off from Your presence, cut off from the light of Your countenance, cut off from Your blessedness just as I have now ritually cut off the foreskin of my flesh."

As a reflection of this sign, the cross represented the supreme act of circumcision. When Jesus took the curse upon Himself, He so identified with our sin that He became a curse. God cut Him off and justly so. This was an act of divine justice. At the moment that Christ took upon Himself the sin of the world, He became the most grotesque, most obscene mass of sin in the history of the world. God is too holy to even look at iniquity. When Christ was hanging on the cross, the Father, as it were, turned His back on Christ. He removed His face. He turned out the lights. He cut off His Son. There was Jesus, who in His human nature had been in a perfect, blessed relationship with God throughout His life. There was Jesus, the Son in whom the Father was well pleased. Now He hung in darkness, isolated from the Father, cut off from fellowship—fully receiving in Himself the curse of God—not for His own sin but for the sin He willingly bore by imputation for our sake.

I have heard many sermons about the physical pain of death by crucifixion. I've heard graphic descriptions of the nails and the thorns. Surely the physical agony of crucifixion was a ghastly thing. But there were thousands who died on crosses and may have had more painful deaths than that of Christ. But only one person has ever received the full measure of the curse of God while on a cross. I doubt that Jesus was even aware of the nails and the spear—He was so overwhelmed by the outer darkness. On the cross Jesus was in the reality of hell. He was totally bereft of the grace and the presence of God, utterly separated from all blessedness of the Father. He became a curse for us so that we someday will be able to see the face of God. So that the light of His countenance might fall upon us, God turned His back on His Son. No wonder Christ screamed. He screamed from the depth of His soul. How long did He have to endure it? We don't know, but a second of it would have been of infinite value.

Finally, Jesus cried, "It is finished!" (John 19:30). It was over. What was over? His life? The pain of the nails? No. It was the forsakenness that ended. The curse was finished. The light of God's countenance returned, and Jesus said, "Into Your hands I commit My spirit" (Luke 23:46). This was a thing incredible. It was a cosmic act of redemption that transcends our full understanding. The imagery of blessing and curse is but the tip of the iceberg. But it was a real curse that brought real redemption.

THE CHARGES AGAINST US: NAILED TO THE CROSS

We have seen that the cross is understood in various ways in the New Testament. In the atonement Christ was the scapegoat who carried our sins away from us (expiation) into the outer darkness. He was the victor over the forces of evil—over principalities and powers. He satisfied the demands of God's justice, paying the ransom in our behalf. He fulfilled the terms of the Old Testament curse. He set the captives free.

The richness of these diverse elements is woven together in summary fashion by Paul in his letter to the Colossians:

> In Him you were also circumcised with the circumcision made without hands, by putting off the body of the sins of the flesh, by the circumcision of Christ, buried with Him in baptism, in which you also were raised with Him through faith in the working of God, who raised Him from the dead. And you, being dead in your trespasses and the uncircumcision of your flesh, He has made alive together with Him, having forgiven you all trespasses, having wiped out the handwriting of requirements that was against us, which was contrary to us. And He has taken it out of the way, having nailed it to the cross. Having disarmed principalities and powers, He made a public spectacle of them, triumphing over them in it (2:11-15).

Paul eloquently speaks of the mystical union between the believer and Christ. We are circumcised with Him. We are also buried with Him so that we will also be raised with Him.

In this text Paul adds another dimension to the multifaceted work of atonement. He writes of Christ's having "wiped out the handwriting of requirements that was against us." What was this handwriting? Before answering, let me relate a personal anecdote.

For Christmas my wife once surprised me with a singular treasure, a gold ring of quite unusual design. It bears the image of Christ on the cross and is capped with a garnet stone that symbolizes the blood of Christ. Above the figure of the cross are the letters INRI. These initials stand for the words "Jesus of Nazareth, King of the Jews" in their Latin form. They recall the gospel account of the crucifixion:

> And an inscription also was written over Him in letters of Greek, Latin, and Hebrew:
>
> THIS IS THE KING OF THE JEWS (Luke 23:38).

The ring my wife gave me is an exact replica of the ring Katharina Von Bora designed and had made for her husband, Martin Luther, on the occasion of their wedding. It symbolizes the gospel, of which I need to be reminded every day.

In the ancient world, when a criminal was charged with a crime, the charges on which he was indicted were formally written down. In like manner, monetary debts were also recorded in writing. When such debts, whether legal or financial, had been paid, a notice to that effect was posted in a prominent public place.

In respect to our indebtedness to God, the handwriting of His requirements that stood against us has been removed from our account by Christ. A notice that the debt has been paid was publicly posted when Jesus was "nailed to the cross." This action is what disarmed the principalities and powers, making a public spectacle of them in Jesus' triumph.

THE BRIDE OF CHRIST: PURCHASED BY HIS BLOOD

One more aspect of the atonement must be mentioned. It has its roots in a somewhat obscure passage in Exodus. In the chapter immediately following the giving of the Ten Commandments we read:

> "Now these are the judgments which you shall set before them: If you buy a Hebrew servant, he shall serve six years; and in the seventh he shall go out free and pay nothing. If he comes in by himself, he shall go out by himself; if he comes in married, then his wife shall go out with him. If his master has given him a wife, and she has borne him sons or daughters, the wife and her children shall be her master's, and he shall go out by himself. But if the servant plainly says, 'I love my master, my wife, and my children; I will not go out free,' then his master shall bring him to the judges. He shall also bring him to the door, or to the door-post, and his master shall pierce his ear with an awl; and he shall serve him forever. And if a man sells his daughter to be a female slave, she shall not go out as the male slaves do. If she does not please her master, who has betrothed her to himself, then he shall let her be redeemed. He shall have no right to sell her to a foreign people, since he has dealt deceitfully with her. And if he has betrothed her to his son, he shall deal with her according to the custom of daugh-

ters. If he takes another wife, he shall not diminish her food, her clothing, and her marriage rights. And if he does not do these three for her, then she shall go out free, without paying money" (Exodus 21:1-11).

This section of the Old Testament law code gives specific provisions regarding indentured servants. Some strange policies are set forth in the text. When the time of release arrived, servants who had entered into service with a wife were released with their wives. But if a servant was single when he came in and thereafter received a wife from his master, when his service was up and he was freed, he was not allowed to take his wife or children out with him. Why not? Presumably because he had not demonstrated that he was able to provide for them. Remember, it was financial indebtedness that had brought him into servitude in the first place. For a man to acquire a wife he had to first pay the "bride price," which demonstrated his ability to care for a family. If the servant wanted to get his wife out of servitude, he had to buy her back. That is, he had to redeem her.

The New Testament looks back to this imagery when it speaks of the church as the Bride of Christ. The church is the Bridegroom's possession. He owns her because He has purchased her. Paul indicates that we are not our own. We are not our own because we have been purchased (1 Corinthians 6:19-20). The purchase price by which we have been bought is the blood of Christ. He in His atoning death has paid the bride price by which His betrothed is redeemed.

7

Appropriating the Cross

THE WORK OF JESUS IN His atonement is directly related to the doctrine of justification. We recall that, during the great controversy of the Protestant Reformation, Martin Luther insisted that the doctrine of justification by faith alone is the article upon which the church stands or falls. During his celebrated debate with Desiderius Erasmus of Rotterdam, as many sparks were flying in the furor of the argument, Luther congratulated Erasmus and thanked him for debating the real issue and not fooling about with trifles. John Calvin agreed with Luther's assessment of the critical importance of justification by faith, arguing that it is the hinge on which everything turns. If these magisterial Reformers were correct, then it is vital for us to understand the relevance of the atonement to our justification.

THE ATONEMENT AND JUSTIFICATION

The issue is, how does the cross of Christ relate to us? We are now finished with the objective question of what happened on the cross, and we turn to the subjective question of how the benefit of Christ's work is appropriated to us. What good is it for us that Christ died on the cross? How does that relate to us? What really happened on the cross? Again, we're talking about the atonement as it relates to the concept of justification. This word *justification* is one of those long, ponderous theological terms that we find in the Bible. But it is at the very heart of the gospel. Sadly, many people in the church have trouble defining the term *justification*.

Let us remember that the need for an atonement is related to the problem of human sin and the character of God—God's holiness and justice. We can illustrate the problem with the following circles.

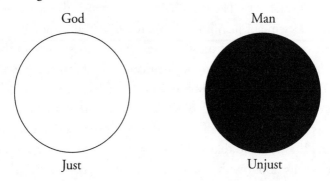

The problem we face is this: God is just, and we are unjust. How are we going to reconcile this conflict between a just and holy God and a fallen, unjust, sinful human being?

To work with this imagery for a minute, let us suppose that the circle on the right represents the character of mankind. If man sins, that sin puts a blemish of sorts, a moral blemish, on the character of fallen man. If he commits another sin, and sin penetrates more deeply into his life, we might add another dot. The issue then becomes, how much of the circle should be shaded when we are judged by the standard of God's perfection? Human corruption is total. It is not that sin touches merely the edges of our lives. It penetrates to the core of our being. Nor is there an island of righteousness preserved in our soul where sin has not reached. Rather, the corruption of sin reaches the whole person.

TOTAL DEPRAVITY AND UTTER DEPRAVITY

There is much misunderstanding about this matter of human corruption. The term that classical Reformed theology often uses for our human predicament is *total depravity.* People have a tendency to wince when we use the term *total depravity,* because there is confusion between the concept of total depravity and the concept of utter depravity. Utter depravity would mean that we are as bad or corrupt as we possibly could be. I don't think that there is a human being in the world who is utterly corrupt. God's restraining grace and power keep us from reaching the realm of utter corruption. Total depravity, by contrast, does not mean that we are as bad as we conceivably could be. As many sins as we have committed, we concede that we could have done worse. We could have committed more gross and heinous sins or sinned more frequently than we actually have.

When the Protestant Reformers talked about total depravity, they meant that sin—its power, its influence, its inclination—affects the *whole* man. Our bodies are fallen. Our hearts are fallen. Our minds are fallen. There is no part of us that escapes the ravages of our sinful human nature. Sin affects our thought life, our conversation, and our behavior. Our whole being is fallen, and that is what we mean by "total depravity."

NO ONE IS RIGHTEOUS

To take it further, when the apostle Paul elaborated on this fallen human condition, he said, "There is none righteous, no, not one. . . . There is none who does good" (Romans 3:10, 12). That is really a radical statement. He was saying that fallen man never does a single good deed. That flies in the face of our experience. We look around us, and we see all kinds of folks who are not Christians doing things that we would applaud for their virtue. We see acts of self-sacrificial heroism, kindness, and charity, for example, among those who are not Christian. Calvin called this *civil righteousness.*

The reason we struggle with the biblical claim that no one does good is that our perspective of the good differs from that of Scripture. First, we must consider the measuring rod of the Law, which is God's measurement of the external performance of human beings. For example, if God says we are not allowed to steal, and we go our whole lives without ever stealing anything, we have kept the Law externally. At least in this outward performance our record is clear.

But in addition to the external measuring rod there is also the consideration of the heart, the internal motivation for our behavior. We judge by outward appearance. God looks on the heart. From a biblical perspective, to do a good deed in the fullest sense of the word requires not only that the deed conform outwardly to the standards of God's Law but that it proceed from a heart that loves Him and wants to honor Him. We remember the great commandment: "You shall love the LORD your God with all your heart" (Matthew 22:37). Let's just stop there for a second. Is there anybody in this world who has loved God with all of his heart for even the last five minutes? No.

Nobody has loved God with all of his heart since being born, nor have we loved Him with all of our mind or strength.

I know that one of the things I will be accountable for on judgment day is the way in which I have failed in the pursuit of the knowledge of God. Many times I have been lazy and slothful and too bored to apply myself to the fullest possible measure of knowing God. I have not loved God with all of my mind. If I loved God with all of my mind, there would never be an impure thought in my head. But that's not the way my head works.

If we considered human performance from God's perspective, we would see why Paul came to that seemingly radical conclusion that there is none righteous, no, not one; that there is none who does good. In the full sense of the word there is no goodness found in fallen people. Even in our finest works there is a taint of sin mixed in. I have never in my life done an act of charity, an act of sacrifice, or act of heroism out of a heart that loved God completely or out of a mind that loved God completely. Externally, all kinds of virtuous acts are going on among both believers and unbelievers. But God considers both the external and the internal. Under that tight norm of judgment, we're in trouble. Because of our sin, our circle becomes completely shaded.

Man

HOW CAN AN UNJUST PERSON
BE MADE RIGHTEOUS?

How is an unjust person going to stand in the presence of God? How can the unjust person be justified? How can the unjust person be made just? Can he start all over again? Can he erase his sin? He cannot. Once a person sins, it is impossible to ever be perfect. He has already lost his perfection by his initial sin. We have a serious problem here. Some may say the problem is not severe because God in His kindness will overlook it. God could do this if He were willing to negotiate His own right-eousness or sacrifice His own justice. But then the Judge of all the earth would not be doing what is right. A judge who does not punish evil is neither just nor good.

Here is where mediation is required. It is at this point that Christ comes to act as our mediator. When we consider our redemption, we tend to think that salvation comes to us sim-ply through the death of Christ. While we are focusing our attention on the death of Christ, it is very easy to overlook something of absolutely crucial significance for the atonement to have any value at all. If I ask a child, "What did Jesus do for you?" the response will be, "Jesus died for my sins." But if that is all Jesus did, then why didn't He just come down from heaven at age thirty and go straight to the cross? The point of the atone-ment is that a just man died for the unjust. But to qualify to be the Redeemer, to qualify to be the Savior, Jesus first had to live a perfect life. He had to live a life of perfect obedience. He had to acquire merit at the bar of justice. What is often over-looked in our justification is that there is a double transaction that takes place.

JUSTIFICATION: A DOUBLE TRANSACTION

Let us illustrate that double transaction. In the circle below representing Jesus, there are no blemishes. He is the One for whom John the Baptist sang the Agnus Dei, "Behold! The Lamb of God who takes away the sin of the world!" (John 1:29). The Lamb of God is the Lamb without blemish. Jesus Himself challenged His enemies to convict Him of sin. None was able to do so. Even at Jesus' trial Pontius Pilate announced that he could find no fault in Him.

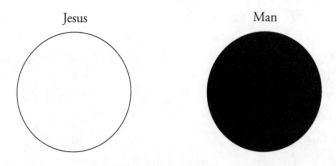

Jesus never flinched from obeying the Law in its fullness. In Him there was no shadow of turning, no blemish, no sin. His "food" was to do the will of the Father (John 4:34). Zeal for His Father's house consumed Him (John 2:17). His passion in life was obedience to the Father. "I do nothing of Myself, but as My Father taught Me, I speak these things. . . . I and the Father are one." It was for these claims that His enemies picked up rocks to attack Him (see John 8:28; 10:30-31).

In the drama of justification we have one unjust party and two just parties. We have a just God, and now we have a just mediator, who is altogether holy. The justification of which the New Testament speaks we call "forensic" justification. Forensics has to do with formal acts of authoritative, legal declaration. "Forensic justification" means that a person is declared to be just at the tribunal of God. The justification takes place ultimately when the supreme Judge of heaven and earth says, "You are just."

The question is, on what possible grounds could God ever say to us, "You are just," when in fact we are not just? Again, how can an unjust person be justified? We find the answer in the biblical concept of imputation. We see it in the imagery of the Lamb of God bearing our sins, just as the Old Testament scapegoat bore the sins of the people. As the priest put his hands on the goat, he was symbolically transferring or imputing the sins of the people to the animal.

Justification: Our Sin Transferred to Christ

In our justification a double transfer takes place. First, the weight of our guilt is transferred to Christ. Christ willingly takes upon Himself all of our sin. Once our sin is imputed to Christ, God sees Him as a mass of corruption. He sees a mass of sinfulness. Because the sin now has been transferred to Jesus' account, He is counted or reckoned guilty in our place.

But if this transfer were all that happened, if the imputation were a one-dimensional transaction, we would never be justified. If Jesus were to take on His back all of the sins that I have ever committed and bear the punishment for me, that would not get me into the kingdom of God. All that would do is keep me out of hell. I would still not be just. I would be innocent but still not just in a positive sense. I would have no righteousness of which to speak. Remember, it is not simply innocence that gets us into the kingdom of God. It is right-eousness. Unless our righteousness exceeds that of the scribes and Pharisees, we will never get into the kingdom of God (see Matthew 5:20). If the only thing that occurred in salvation were the removal of my guilt, I would still have no merit.

Justification: Christ's Righteousness Transferred to Us

So there is a double transfer. Not only is the sin of mankind imputed to Christ, but His righteousness is transferred to our account. In God's sight our circle is now clean. When God declares me just, He is not lying. This is no mere legal fiction.

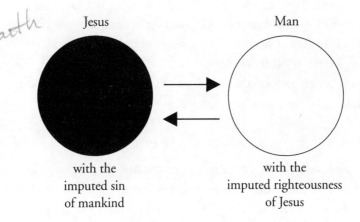

Faith

Jesus

with the
imputed sin
of mankind

Man

with the
imputed righteousness
of Jesus

If the imputation were fictional, then God's declaration would be a legal fiction. It would be a lie and blemish on the character of God. But the point of the gospel is that the impu-tation is real. God really did lay my sins on Christ, and God really did transfer Christ's righteousness to me. There is a gen-uine union for those who are in Christ. We truly possess the righteousness of Jesus Christ by imputation. Christ is our righteousness. That's why He is our Savior: not merely because He died but because He lived. Without His meritorious life the atonement would have no value. Without His obedience, His suffering on the cross would be merely a tragedy. We must have the double transfer, by which God declares us just.

Faith

When we consider this double imputation, we see the essence of our salvation in a phrase made famous by Martin Luther: *simul justus et peccator. Simul* is the Latin word from which we get the English word simultaneous. It means "at the same time." *Justus* is the word for "just" or "righteous." *Et* means "and." *Peccator* is the Latin word for sinner. So *simul justus et peccator* means "at the same time just and sinner." This is the glory of the doctrine of justification by faith alone. The person who is in Christ is at the very same instant both just and a sinner. That's good news, for if I had to wait until there was no sin in me to get into the kingdom of God, I would surely never make it.

JUSTIFICATION: BY CHRIST ALONE

The whole point of the gospel is that the minute I embrace Jesus Christ, all that Christ has done is applied to me. All that He is becomes mine, including His righteousness. Luther's phrase "at the same time just and sinner" means that, at the very instant that I believe, I am just by virtue of the imputation of Christ's righteousness. It is Christ's righteousness that makes me just. His death has taken care of the punishment I deserve. His life has made possible my eternal reward. There it is. My justice is all tied up in Christ. And yet at the same time, in and of myself I am a sinner. It is sinners who are saved by the atonement. That is the glory of the gospel and of the cross. The Bible tells us that the only way we can have the righteousness and the merit of Christ transferred to our account is by faith. We cannot earn it. We cannot deserve it. We cannot merit it. We can only trust in it and cling to it.

Justification by faith alone means very simply this. Justification is by Christ alone. It is by His merit, His righteousness, His life, His death that we can stand in the presence of a holy God. Without Christ we are without hope because all we can ever offer to God is our "unjustness."

No wonder the author of Hebrews asked, "How shall we escape if we neglect so great a salvation?" (Hebrews 2:3). That is a rhetorical question. The answer to the question is obvious. How will we escape? We will not. We cannot, because it is impossible for an unjust person to survive in the presence of a just God. We need to be justified. We're going to seek justification either through our own righteousness or through what the Reformers called a "foreign righteousness." And the only foreign righteousness available for us is the righteousness of Christ.

faith

Double trans action of Atonement

1. Christ died for the forgiveness of our sin

2. Christ died imputing His righteousness to us, making us righteous (sinless before Father)

we must have both to receive salvation

PART III

Saved *for* What?

8

Adoption and the
Beatific Vision

FOR SEVERAL YEARS I have been the teacher on a nation-
ally broadcast radio program called "Renewing Your Mind."
The program airs daily around the country but is taped in
advance. We tape the messages before a live audience, a small
group of about thirty people who come to our studio in
Orlando. One couple had attended these tapings from the
beginning. We often held sessions twice a week, doing three or
four lectures per session. They were present for all of the sessions. Since we frequently had visitors, I would begin by going
around the room and asking people to introduce themselves.
When I came to the couple I've mentioned, the husband would
say simply, "My name is Harold Schellenberg, and I'm happy
to be here." Then his face would burst into a huge grin.

Harold became seriously ill. He was diagnosed with multi-
ple brain tumors and the prognosis was that his illness was ter-
minal. The cancer was a virulent type and quickly left Harold
in a debilitated condition. It seemed that he lost more strength
each day. Soon he was able to do very little. Yet his devoted

wife, Eve, cared for him every moment. She brought him to the tapings every week in a wheelchair. In the final weeks of his illness he lost his sight. Still he came to the tapings. He continued to introduce himself in the same manner. Still he graced us all with his infectious smile. Harold was one of the kindest, sweetest people I have ever known. He didn't know how to complain. Near the end I would ask him, "Harold, how are you doing?" He would reply, "I'm okay, because the Lord's taking care of me."

Harold loved the Scripture. He loved the church. It was fitting that he died on a Sunday. The Sabbath day was the day he entered his rest. I imagine that the moment he breathed his last, there was an instant transition from this world into glory. He stepped through the great dimensional barrier into the immediate presence of Christ, experiencing, as Paul says, how much better it is "to be absent from the body and to be present with the Lord" (2 Corinthians 5:8). It was my great privilege to give the eulogy at Harold's funeral. At the conclusion I could not resist speculation about his entrance into heaven. I was convinced that the second he stepped into glory, he looked into the face of Jesus and said, "Hi, my name is Harold Schellenberg, and I'm happy to be here."

TO LIVE IS CHRIST, TO DIE IS GAIN

It is a precious thing to watch a saint die. The death of saints is sweet in the eyes of God. We get all sorts of advice on how to live, but few lessons on how to die. The Puritans, on the other hand, were concerned not only about holy living but also about holy dying. We have a tendency to forget that the goal of our whole lives points beyond the grave. We sing the gospel song, "This world is not my home, I'm just a passing through." But as we pass through this life, we often let our gaze wander away from our goal. We cling tenaciously to this life as if it were better than what lies ahead. Our attitude is rarely that expressed by Paul when he wrote,

> For I know that this will turn out for my deliverance through your prayer and the supply of the Spirit of Jesus Christ, according to my earnest expectation and hope that in nothing I shall be ashamed, but with all boldness, as always, so now also Christ will be magnified in my body, whether by life or by death. For to me, to live is Christ, and to die is gain. But if I live on in the flesh, this will mean fruit from my labor; yet what I shall choose I cannot tell. For I am hard-pressed between the two, having a desire to depart and be with Christ, which is far better. Nevertheless to remain in the flesh is more needful for you (Philippians 1:19-24).

Paul is torn by ambivalence. He is caught between two opposite yearnings. On the one hand, he wants to leave this world. He is ready for his departure. On the other hand, he is pressed to stay on in order to meet the needs of his congregations. Notice that his comparison of the two states he contemplates is not between the good and the bad. Neither is it between the good and the better. It is the difference between the good and the *far* better.

Paul does not denigrate this life. This life is good, and we seek to enjoy it to the fullest. This is my Father's world, and I am not to despise it. In this world I do not experience the absence of God, for Christ sent His Holy Spirit to be His presence for us here. But there is a new dimension to the presence of Christ when we pass through the veil. Then we enter directly into His *immediate* presence.

Again we notice that Paul is not in a quandary simply between living and dying. Rather it is between leaving and staying. He doesn't want to leave just to be rid of this world and its afflictions. He is not looking for an escape hatch. He wants to depart so that he can be with Christ. That is his deepest desire.

ENTERING INTO THE PRESENCE OF CHRIST

The promise of entering into Christ's presence came initially from the lips of Jesus Himself. In His Upper Room discourse to His disciples Jesus said:

> "Let not your heart be troubled; you believe in God, believe also in Me. In My Father's house are many mansions; if it were not so, I would have told you. I go to prepare a place for you. And if I go and prepare a place for you, I will come again and receive you to Myself; that where I am, there you may be also. And where I go you know, and the way you know" (John 14:1-4).

Jesus' command to His friends was that they not allow their hearts to be troubled. He spoke of the many mansions in His Father's house. As He was about to leave His friends, He assured them that He was going ahead of them to make preparations for the time they would rejoin Him. He promised that where He was, they would be too.

These comforting words were further enhanced later in the discourse when Jesus said,

> "These things I have spoken to you while being present with you. But the Helper, the Holy Spirit, whom the Father will

send in My name, He will teach you all things, and bring to your remembrance all things that I said to you. Peace I leave with you, My peace I give to you; not as the world gives do I give to you. Let not your heart be troubled, neither let it be afraid. You have heard Me say to you, 'I am going away and coming back to you.' If you loved Me, you would rejoice because I said, 'I am going to the Father,' for My Father is greater than I" (John 14:25-28).

ADOPTED IN CHRIST

Heaven, our destination, is inseparably linked to our adoption in Christ. We are promised rooms in our Father's house because we have been adopted into our Father's family. As His family members, we become His heirs. Paul describes our adoption in Romans 8:14-18:

> For as many as are led by the Spirit of God, these are sons of God. For you did not receive the spirit of bondage again to fear, but you received the Spirit of adoption by whom we cry out, "Abba, Father." The Spirit Himself bears witness with our spirit that we are children of God, and if children, then heirs—heirs of God and joint heirs with Christ, if indeed we suffer with Him, that we may also be glorified together. For I consider that the sufferings of this present time are not worthy to be compared with the glory which shall be revealed in us.

The linkage between our adoption in Christ and our future blessedness in heaven is declared in 1 John 3:1-3:

> Behold what manner of love the Father has bestowed on us, that we should be called children of God! Therefore the world does not know us, because it did not know Him. Beloved, now we are children of God; and it has not yet been revealed what

we shall be, but we know that when He is revealed, we shall
be like Him, for we shall see Him as He is. And everyone
who has this hope in Him purifies himself, just as He is pure.

John calls attention to the end or purpose for which we are made.
He declares our highest point of glory—the very acme of our salvation. He begins with the word "Behold." It is a summons to
pay close attention. It is a call to stop and rivet our attention on
what is about to come. John is writing to the church when he
says, "Look . . . behold what manner of love . . ." He stops us in
our tracks. He asks us to consider the specific type or category
of love that is revealed in our salvation. We could take the category of "love" and divide it into numerous different species:
there is puppy love, erotic love, romantic love . . . and there is
spiritual love. We can examine all the varieties of love, but John
says, "Wait a minute. What kind of love is this, that we should
be called the children of God?"

"PEACE, BE STILL"

There is something similar in this inquiry, in terms of intensity, to a question raised by the disciples in a boat on the Sea of
Galilee after a storm (see Mark 4:35-41). Jesus had been rest-
ing in the back of the boat when violent turbulence erupted
without warning. The winds came down off the Mediterranean
and stirred up the waters. His disciples, seasoned veterans, were
afraid that they were going to perish. In their terror they came
and awakened Jesus, pleading, "Lord, do something or we perish." We know what happened. Jesus assessed the situation. He
looked at the fury of the blowing wind and the waves that were
threatening to capsize the boat. Then He did something amaz-

ing. The incarnate Creator of wind and water, in a manner reminiscent of the divine imperative of creation itself, gave a verbal command to the elements, saying, "Peace, be still." Instantly the sea was as glass. There was not even the slightest zephyr or whisper of wind in the air—absolute calmness. We would expect that with the calming of the sea, there would have been a corresponding calming of the fears and anxiety of the disciples. But that is not what happened. The Bible tells us, "And they became very much afraid." After the immediate threat had been removed, the disciples' terror increased. Why? Suddenly they were paralyzed in the grip of xenophobia, the fear of strangers. They realized they were in the presence of the ultimate alien.

What does one do upon encountering someone who can talk to the wind and the sea and command instant obedience? The disciples experienced terror because this alien was far more threatening to them than was the sea. "Behold, what manner of man is this?" (see Mark 4:41, KJV). They had no category that would capture or contain Jesus. He was in a class by Himself. Because He was in this extraordinary class, He terrified them. The manner of man that He was transcended any other type of human they had ever experienced. In similar fashion John utters his astonishment at the adopting love of God: "Behold what manner of love the Father has bestowed on us, that we should be called children of God!" We don't have a category for that kind of love. There is nothing common or ordinary about it.

THE ASTONISHING REALITY OF OUR ADOPTION

It seems that in our day we have been inoculated against such amazement. We have been immunized to the astonishing reality of our adoption. We have been told over and over that we are all God's children. We assume that God is our Father by nature.

By no means! The Bible asserts that by nature we are children of wrath. There is no universal fatherhood of God or universal brotherhood of man. The Bible speaks of a universal *neighborhood*. All people are my neighbors, and I am to treat them with Christian love. But not all people are my brothers and sisters. That kinship comes only by adoption. Jesus is God's only natural Son. All others enter His family through adoption in Christ.

The assumptions of people living in the first century were different from ours. Being children of God was not assumed. Indeed it was a radical idea. For John it was incredible that the Lord God omnipotent would look at us and call us family.

We get a glimpse of the radical graciousness of adoption in the Old Testament account of the fate of Mephibosheth, the lame son of Jonathan. After the deaths of Saul and Jonathan, the zealous generals of David scoured the land to destroy any possible survivors from Saul's family who might prove to be hostile rivals for the throne that was being transferred to David. The purge was not David's idea. He had no desire to exact vengeance from the house of Saul. When the report of Saul's and Jonathan's deaths came in, David mourned. He lamented over their demise and composed the "Song of the Bow," which he instructed should be taught to the children of Judah:

> "The beauty of Israel is slain on your high places!
> How the mighty have fallen!
>   Tell it not in Gath,
> Proclaim it not in the streets of Ashkelon—
> Lest the daughters of the Philistines rejoice,

Lest the daughters of the uncircumcised triumph.
O mountains of Gilboa,
Let there be no dew nor rain upon you,
Nor fields of offerings.
For the shield of the mighty is cast away there!
The shield of Saul, not anointed with oil.
    From the blood of the slain,
From the fat of the mighty,
The bow of Jonathan did not turn back,
And the sword of Saul did not return empty.
Saul and Jonathan were beloved and pleasant in their lives,
And in their death they were not divided;
They were swifter than eagles,
They were stronger than lions" (2 Samuel 1:19-23).

This lament reveals David's profound love for Jonathan.
Verse 26 reads:

"I am distressed for you, my brother Jonathan;
You have been very pleasant to me;
Your love to me was wonderful,
Surpassing the love of women."

Because of his love for Jonathan, David asked if there were
any survivors from the family. There were rumors of a lone
survivor, a boy named Mephibosheth who was crippled in both
legs and who had been secreted away into hiding. So the soldiers
of David went on a search mission throughout the land. Finally
Mephibosheth was discovered. We can imagine the terror of
the woman who was his guardian when the knock came at the
door. The thing she had feared most was now taking place as the
soldiers burst into the home. The soldiers seized Mephibosheth.
Surely the boy was equally terrorized. I imagine him crying

and pleading for help. He had no real idea of his actual destiny, only a gruesome anticipation of being executed. When he was brought into Jerusalem, the soldiers took him to David. The Bible records the encounter:

> Now when Mephibosheth the son of Jonathan, the son of Saul, had come to David, he fell on his face and prostrated himself. Then David said, "Mephibosheth?" And he answered, "Here is your servant!" So David said to him, "Do not fear, for I will surely show you kindness for Jonathan your father's sake, and will restore to you all the land of Saul your grandfather; and you shall eat bread at my table continually." Then he bowed himself, and said, "What is your servant, that you should look upon such a dead dog as I?" And the king called to Ziba, Saul's servant, and said to him, "I have given to your master's son all that belonged to Saul and to all his house. You therefore, and your sons and your servants, shall work the land for him, and you shall bring in the harvest, that your master's son may have food to eat. But Mephibosheth your master's son shall eat bread at my table always." Now Ziba had fifteen sons and twenty servants. Then Ziba said to the king, "According to all that my lord the king has commanded his servant, so will your servant do." "As for Mephibosheth," said the king, "he shall eat at my table like one of the king's sons" (2 Samuel 9:6-11).

The text indicates that Mephibosheth was not given the privilege of eating at the king's table only occasionally. Rather he ate *continually* at the king's table and was treated as one of the king's sons.

This is a vivid illustration of what it means to be adopted into the family of God. Every time I go to the Lord's Supper I think of this. I realize I am coming to the King's table as a spiritual cripple whose soul is powerless to please Him. I come help-less, save for the help of my older brother Jesus, who brings me into the family of God.

GOD'S IMMEASURABLE LOVE

It was not because David had great affection for Mephibosheth that he invited him to the king's table. He didn't even know him. Why did he do it? He did it because of his love for Jonathan. I can think of no reason why any of us are in the family of God, other than that the Father has been determined from the foundation of the world that His Son would "see the labor of His soul, and be satisfied" (Isaiah 53:11). We are, as Christ indicates in John 17, the ones the Father has given to the Son. It is because of the immeasurable love that the Father has for His Son that we are called the children of God. Because the Father loves our older brother, we have been adopted into His family and have been seated at His table.

We must never take this unspeakable privilege for granted. Every time we pray and address God as "Father," we should think of the extraordinary love that makes this filial address possible. John says, "Behold what manner of love the Father has bestowed on us, that we should be called children of God! Therefore the world does not know us, because it did not know Him."

STRANGERS AND ALIENS IN THIS WORLD

To be a member of the family of God is no longer to be a stranger to Him. We are now known of God. Now, we become aliens to the very world from which we have come. If we are

Christians, the way we think is now foreign to the ways of this world. The world cannot possibly understand us.

There is a certain dimension of the Christian mind that pagans can never understand as long as they are within the context of paganism. The Bible says that "the world does not know us, because it did not know Him" (1 John 3:1). Since we have been engrafted into Christ's body and adopted into His house, the alienation and estrangement of the world from Him is transferred to us. This is one of the problems that tempts us to compromise. It hurts us when the world rejects us. We still want everyone to love us. We deeply desire the applause of our fellow man. We don't particularly enjoy being associated with the humiliation of Christ.

Have you been baptized? Into what were you baptized? Have you been baptized into the death of Christ? Have you been baptized into the resurrection of Christ? If you have been baptized, you have received a mark on your soul. It is an indelible mark that brands you as one whom God has set apart to participate in the humiliation of Christ. If we are not willing to participate in the humiliation of Christ, we will never participate in the exaltation of Christ. But if we are willing to participate in the shame of Christ, we will also participate in the glory of Christ. We bear that mark in our bodies in the sign of baptism. We are identified with Christ. As a result, the world does not know us because it did not know Him.

WHAT WILL WE BE LIKE IN HEAVEN?

John goes on and says, "Beloved, now we are children of God; and it has not yet been revealed what we shall be" (1 John 3:2a). There is a crucial contrast here. It is a contrast between what we know about the present and what we *don't* know about the *future*. In terms of the present, this much we know. Right now, we are the children of God. That much we know, says John. But we don't know exactly what we will be like in the future. People occasionally ask me, "What am I going to be like in heaven? Am I going to be fifty-eight forever? Is my new body going to be overweight? Am I going to recover the moves that I had when I was eighteen years old?" I am amazed by these questions—that anybody might think I would be able to answer them! There are things we do not yet know.

We don't know exactly what we're going to be like in heaven. For years after my father's death I was besieged with a recurring nightmare. His death had been a slow one. He deteriorated over a three-year period. He died an inch at a time, suffering several debilitating strokes. After a while he was paralyzed and his hair had turned pure white. He was only fifty-two years old, but he looked eighty. He sat in his chair every day until dinnertime. Then I would come and bend down in front of him with my back toward him. I would take his lifeless arms and wrap them around my neck, hoist him up on my back, and pull him. His feet would drag uselessly as I carried him into the dining room and lowered him into his chair. To maintain his dignity he wanted to sit at the table for dinner. His vision was almost gone, and his speech was slurred. But still, as long as he was alive, he wanted to sit at the head of the table for dinner. When dinner was finished, I would repeat the process and drag him back to his room.

When he died, it was as if my soul died with him. From a teenage boy's perspective, I thought he was the greatest man that ever lived. After he died, for years I kept having a terrible nightmare that would wake me up in a cold sweat. In the nightmare, my father would appear. Every time my emotions were the same. I would be so excited to see him. Then my joy would turn to despair, because he was in the same condition as when he was dying. In the dream I knew there was no hope. He was dying, and there was nothing I could do to stop it. Those dreams stopped about twenty years ago. But before they stopped, I had had that same dream at least thirty times. And then it stopped, and I never dreamed about my father again until about three years ago.

We have all sorts of dreams. Why we dream what we do is anybody's guess. Psychiatrists may guess at their significance, but dream interpretation is not an exact science. Some dreams are so vivid and intense that in the morning we can remember them exactly. My last dream of my father was one of these. I don't believe for a second that it was some new revelation from God. All I know for sure is that it was a dream. But it got my attention.

In this dream my father appeared for the first time with a perfect body. I recognized him instantly, but I had no idea how old he was. His face was bronzed and sun-tanned. His features were powerful, but I couldn't tell whether he was forty-five or twenty-five. There was no way to guess his age. This time he did not have the appearance of someone who was dying. There was a kind of radiance to him. And I said, "Dad, you're alive!"

He looked at me with a twinkle in his eyes. He smiled and said, "Of course, I'm alive. What did you think?"

And I responded, "But you have your new body, and I didn't think we would get that until a long time from now."

And he said, "Well, I have it already."

And I replied, "Okay."

I was not going to argue theology with my father if he was already there. I asked, "Dad, what was it like the first time you saw Jesus?"

He said, "Oh, Son, it's just like in the book of Revelation. There are no lamps. There are no lights there. There's no sun and there's no moon. The whole place is illumined by the glory of God and by the Lamb." He continued, "And, Son, when I first saw the dazzling glory of Christ, it was just incredible."

And I said, "You mean you saw it just once, and then you had to go to some other corner of heaven and merely remember it?"

He answered, "No, the incredible thing is that it doesn't matter where you are in heaven; you can see Him as He is."

"WE SHALL SEE HIM AS HE IS"

That was my dream. It was a dream that connected the greatest pain of my life—the loss of my father—with the greatest hope of my life—the New Testament promise of the Beatific Vision, the *visio Dei*. I don't think I have ever in my life heard a sermon on the Beatific Vision, and I cannot fathom why. It is the ultimate prize, the ultimate goal for the Christian. The word *beatific* comes from the same root from which we get the word *beatitude*. Thus the Beatific Vision is a vision of supreme blessedness, the blessedness we will experience when we see God face to face.

John continues:

> Now we are children of God; and it has not yet been revealed
> what we shall be, but we know that when He is revealed,
> we shall be like Him, for we shall see Him as He is. And
> everyone who has this hope in Him purifies himself, just as
> He is pure (1 John 3:2-3).

There is a serious question in this text—a question that has occupied the minds of theologians over the centuries. It's a "chicken or the egg" type of question. John tells us that we shall see God as He is (in the Latin, *in se est*). The idea here is that we are going to see God, not the way He would appear in a cloud of shekinah glory, not in a burning bush, not in the pillar of smoke of the Old Testament, not by way of theophany, not by way of outward appearances. God is a spirit. We are going to see Him in His essence.

But how can we see a spirit in its essence?

For that matter, how can I see anyone? For me to see anything, I have to have a body. I have to have eyes. There has to be light. There has to be something physical for me to see—something illumined by the light. Vision involves a dynamic of all kinds of chemistry and physics. Light reflects off the object, an image comes to me, and it strikes me in the eyes. It goes through the pupil, lens, and retina, and all the parts that connect to the optic nerve. It is through this complicated process that an image appears on the screen of my mind. And I think I've just seen an object. But what I've seen is some kind of an image of photons and all the rest. My entire visionary experience is mediated through the senses and nerve endings.

If God is a Spirit and has no body, how will we ever be able to see Him? Jonathan Edwards suggested that when a soul perceives a spirit, there is no transfer of images (or photons). No optic nerve or lens is required. When the soul has a direct perception of God, it is an "immediate" experience.

What do we mean by an "immediate" experience?

Let me illustrate. At the end of the football season I ask people, "Did you see the Super Bowl?" When they answer in the affirmative, I ask detailed questions, for instance, how warm was it in the stadium? Then they usually qualify their original answer by saying that they saw the Super Bowl on television. In reality they did not see the Super Bowl. They viewed a televised broadcast through the transmission of light images. Or they read about the Super Bowl in the newspaper, or heard it on the radio. In a word, they had a "mediated" version of the Super Bowl. Their contact with the actual Super Bowl came through some aspect of what we call the "media."

The media are so called because they represent some "medium," something that stands between us and the actual reality they report to us. But even when we are eyewitnesses of real events, our perceptions of those events are mediated to our minds through our physical senses.

Imagine having an unmediated, direct apprehension of the very being of God. That is what the New Testament promises will occur at the end of the Christian's earthly life. We don't yet know what we're going to be. But we know this: we're going to be like Him, and we're going to see Him as He is.

SEEING THE PURE GLORY OF GOD

Let us return to our "chicken or the egg" question. The Bible tells us that the end of our sanctification will be our glorification, when all vestigial remnants of sin will be removed from our character. We will be pure. No more doubt. No more fear. No more error. No more pain. No more evil. All of these things will be gone forever. We will be like Christ, totally sanctified. We will see Him as He is in His unveiled splendor and glory. We will see something that will dwarf the vision Isaiah had of the Holy One.

Here is the question: are we going to be able to see Him because God will first purify us and glorify us, making it possible for us to see Him? The reason why we are not able to see God now is not a deficiency in our eyes. The problem is with our hearts. God will not allow Himself to be seen by anybody who is anything less than pure in heart. We recall that Jesus pronounced His blessing on the pure of heart, promising that they would see God. We are not pure in heart. Therefore, we cannot see beyond our present dimension. We can see things in three dimensions but not beyond. We are unable to penetrate into the realm of supernature. We cannot see into the realm of God because we are not *allowed* to see into the realm of God. There still is an angel at the doorway to paradise with a flaming sword that bars access. No human being shall see God and live. We are not going to be able to see Him until we are purified. So is this what happens: God purifies us, and then the lights come on, and we bask in the immediate apprehension of the glory of Christ? I am not sure.

Perhaps what happens follows a different sequence. Maybe it is not that we are first purified and then are able to see God's unveiled glory. Maybe what happens is that God reveals His pure glory to us. The very sight of Him may be the power that He uses to perfect us, and we are purified by the vision. I don't know which comes first. I really don't care which comes first. What I want is to see Him. What I want is for all those who embrace Christ to someday have their eyes opened—the eyes of their soul—that they may see the holy glory of Jesus Christ unveiled. That is what we were made for. That is what we sense is missing in the deepest chambers of our souls. This is the hollow ache that must be healed before we can attain the fulfillment of our purpose as human beings. Nothing less will do.

This is the destiny God promises His people. This is the goal and purpose of our salvation. This is what we are saved *for*. We are saved *by* God, *from* God, *for* God. That is the full irony of the drama of salvation.

A New Heaven and a New Earth

Finally, we read of God's promise of a new heaven and a new earth, the promise of a New Jerusalem that will descend from heaven itself. This is the capstone of the revelation that John received while exiled on the Isle of Patmos:

> Now I saw a new heaven and a new earth, for the first heaven and the first earth had passed away. Also there was no more sea. Then I, John, saw the holy city, New Jerusalem, coming down out of heaven from God, prepared as a bride adorned for her husband. And I heard a loud voice from heaven saying, "Behold, the tabernacle of God is with men, and He will dwell with them, and they shall be His people. God Himself will be with them and be their God. And God will wipe away every tear from their eyes; there shall be no more death, nor sorrow, nor crying. There shall be no more pain, for the former things have passed away." Then He who sat on the throne said, "Behold, I make all things new." And He said to me, "Write, for these words are true and faithful." And He said to me, "It is done! I am the Alpha and the Omega, the Beginning and the End. I will give of the fountain of the water of life freely to him

who thirsts. He who overcomes shall inherit all things, and I will be his God and he shall be My son" (Revelation 21:1-7).

John describes in terms of streets of gold, gates of pearls, and walls adorned with precious stones the heavenly city to which we are given title by Christ. He describes a city of such magnificent beauty that it makes the most majestic human constructions of this world appear as blighted slums in contrast.

This city has no church. No spires or steeples mark its skyline. No temple is present because in this place none is needed:

> But I saw no temple in it, for the Lord God Almighty and the Lamb are its temple. The city had no need of the sun or of the moon to shine in it, for the glory of God illuminated it. The Lamb is its light. And the nations of those who are saved shall walk in its light, and the kings of the earth bring their glory and honor into it. Its gates shall not be shut at all by day (there shall be no night there). And they shall bring the glory and the honor of the nations into it (Revelation 21:22-26).

SO GREAT A SALVATION

Finally, in the last chapter of the Bible, John describes a pure river—a river of the water of life, clear as crystal. It is in this majestic setting that our Beatific Vision will take place. It is here that the ultimate chapter of our salvation will be written:

> And he showed me a pure river of water of life, clear as crystal, proceeding from the throne of God and of the Lamb. In the middle of its street, and on either side of the river, was the tree of life, which bore twelve fruits, each tree yield-

ing its fruit every month. The leaves of the tree were for the healing of the nations. And there shall be no more curse, but the throne of God and of the Lamb shall be in it, and His servants shall serve Him. They shall see His face, and His name shall be on their foreheads. There shall be no night there: They need no lamp nor light of the sun, for the Lord God gives them light. And they shall reign forever and ever (Revelation 22:1-5).

How then shall we escape if we neglect so great a salvation? It is a salvation that is *by* God, *from* God, and *for* God, to whom belongs all glory.

General Index

Scripture Index